PRAISE FOR COMFORT FOR THE GRIEVING PARENT'S HEART

"Gary Roe is no stranger to grief. In *Comfort for the Grieving Parent's Heart*, he captures the silent anguish of the grieving and provides practical understanding and insight for how to deal with grief. I found myself saying, 'YES, YES, YES!' with every page. If you find yourself in the midst of grief, this is a must read to help make sense of it all."

– Dr. Troy Allen, Pastor

"The author's ability to connect with the grieving parent's heart is so evident in this book. Readers will see themselves on almost every page and find the comfort they need in Gary's compassionate empathy and counsel. I highly recommend this book to anyone experiencing the loss of a child, no matter what age."

– Paul Casale,
Licensed Professional Counselor/Marriage and Family Therapist

"Healing from the loss of a child is hard work. To do it well, we need to engage the bereavement challenge every day. In *Comfort for the Grieving Parent's Heart*, Gary guides the reader through the healing process with a daily dose of honesty, courage, compassion and love."

– Dr. Craig Borchardt,
President / CEO, Hospice Brazos Valley

"I give this book the highest praise I can – it rings true. While reading it, I relived the range of emotions I felt through my grief journey. At the end I felt hopeful and light again, just like in real life. I know it will be a treasured resource for others."

– Kelli Levey Reynolds,
Mays Business School, Texas A & M University

"If you're struggling with the loss of a child, be encouraged. Gary's book, *Comfort for the Grieving Parent's Heart*, walks you through the process of emotional healing. You'll find hope, healing, and help filtering your feelings."

– Dr. Charles W. Page, MD

"*Comfort for the Grieving Parent's Heart* is the book for anyone who loses a child. In its chapters you'll recognize how you're feeling that day, gain insight into why you're feeling that way, and learn strategies to cope and grow. You'll return to it again and again."

– Debra Johnson,
M.Div., Hospice Bereavement Coordinator

"In his new book, *Comfort for the Grieving Parent's Heart*, Gary Roe masterfully describes the journey of grief after losing a child. But he doesn't stop there. He guides the reader to a deeper understanding of what they may face on their journey. Then he provides helpful insights and affirmations to assist them along the way. There are no simple or correct paths on the grief journey. That is why *Comfort for the Grieving Parent's Heart* is a must read. It will assist the reader in maneuvering the potholes, detours and dead ends they may face along this road."

– Brian Kenney, Pastor

"From the first words on the first pages, I knew that this book was going to be different. This isn't just a book about grieving. It's about me. How am I going to heal? Where is my hope? Gary is speaking directly into my soul. Every page tells me that it's somehow going to be okay."

– Scott Marlow,
Journey Church

"In *Comfort for the Grieving Parent's Heart*, Gary masterfully describes the tapestry of emotion experienced by those affected by the loss of a child. His connection to the reader is demonstrated through sharing his own journey of loss and healing. I share his books with clients and friends with great confidence."

– Carrie Andree,
Licensed Professional Counselor

"Gary Roe seems to have the ability to put into words exactly what my heart felt. His writings are full of truth and healing. Thank you, Gary, for using your personal pain to help others on their grief journey."

– Page Bratcher,
Grief and Divorce Recovery Coach

"An easy to read book with short, daily chapters. The format offers a unique way to deal with grief. I especially like the affirmations at the end of each chapter. Be sure to read the Summary of Grief Affirmations at the end of the book."

– Cindy Fanning,
LMSW, Hospice Bereavement Coordinator

COMFORT FOR THE *Grieving* PARENT'S HEART

HOPE AND HEALING AFTER LOSING YOUR CHILD

GARY ROE

Comfort for the Grieving Parent's Heart

First Edition: April 2020
ISBN: 978-1-950382-31-6

Formatting: Streetlight Graphics

Published by: Healing Resources Publishing

Thank you for purchasing *Comfort for the Grieving Parent's Heart.*

These pages are designed to be a companion
for you in your grief journey.

Please don't read this book just once.

Pick it up again in six months or a year.

Come to it again and again.

Each time you will be at a different place.

You'll see your progress. You'll be encouraged.

And you'll find your hope has grown.

As a thanks, please accept this gift – an exclusive,
free, printable PDF for readers of this book.

Download yours today:
Healing Affirmations for Grieving Hearts
https://www.garyroe.com/healing-affirmations-for-grieving-hearts/

OTHER BOOKS BY GARY ROE

The Comfort Series

Comfort for the Grieving Heart: Hope and Encouragement in Times of Loss

Comfort for the Grieving Spouse's Heart: Hope and Healing After Losing Your Partner

Comfort for the Grieving Adult Child's Heart: Hope and Healing After Losing Your Parent

The Difference Maker Series

Difference Maker: Overcoming Adversity and Turning Pain into Purpose, Every Day (Adult and Teen Editions)

Living on the Edge: How to Fight and Win the Battle for Your Mind and Heart (Adult and Teen Editions)

Teen Grief: Caring for the Grieving Teenage Heart

Shattered: Surviving the Loss of a Child

Please Be Patient, I'm Grieving: How to Care for and Support the Grieving Heart

Heartbroken: Healing from the Loss of a Spouse

Surviving the Holidays Without You: Navigating Grief During Special Seasons

Saying Goodbye: Facing the Loss of a Loved One (co-author)

Not Quite Healed: 40 Truths for Male Survivors of Childhood Sexual Abuse (co-author)

TABLE OF CONTENTS

WHAT THIS BOOK IS ALL ABOUT

COMFORT.

We need it. Badly.

Loss is painful. Separation hurts. When a child departs, our worlds change.

We've known them all their lives. They've never taken a single breath without us being present somehow.

Or perhaps we adopted them. We received and loved them not because we had to, but because we wanted to. We chose them.

Maybe it's a stepchild we've lost, but we embraced them as our own. Love is powerful and can transcend any obstacle or boundary.

Not all familial relationships are close. Perhaps our deceased child was a challenge for us to relate to and get along with. If they were an adult, maybe we were even estranged from them due to circumstances or wounds in the past.

No matter what the situation or how close the relationship, the loss of a child is shocking and traumatic. Our world shifted when they took their last breath. It all feels backwards. It feels wrong.

Oblivious to our suffering, the world around us speeds on as if nothing happened. Stunned, shocked, sad, confused, and angry, we blink in disbelief. The pain can be immense.

We long for comfort. We look for it. Grieving moms and dads need it to survive.

In my own grief, I have been comforted by the compassion and kindness of others. Over the decades as a missionary and pastor, and now as a hospice chaplain and grief counselor, I've had the honor of walking with thousands of grieving hearts through the valley of loss, offering what comfort I can along the way. This is how comfort works. We comfort others with the comfort we ourselves have received.

HOW TO READ THIS BOOK

This book is about comfort. The loss of a child is tragic and devastating. My desire is to meet you where you are in your pain and walk with you there.

Comfort for the Grieving Parent's Heart is designed to be read one chapter each day, giving you bite-sized bits of comfort over time. You do not have to read it this way, of course. You may find yourself wanting to read the same chapter several days in a row, or perhaps go back and reread a chapter here and there. We all grieve differently. Read in the way that is most natural for you.

The grieving process does not follow a formula of ordered steps. Instead, grief often comes in waves from multiple directions. We can experience various emotions and seemingly conflicting thoughts all at once. As result, I have not numbered these chapters because I don't want to give the impression that grief is an orderly and predictable process. It is more like a meandering path strewn with unforeseen obstacles.

Chapters are purposefully brief and easy-to-read. Each chapter begins with the Grieving Heart speaking, followed by some thoughts about that day's subject (shock, sadness, confusion, anger, anxiety, etc.). Every reading ends with an affirmation. I have compiled these affirmations for you at the end of the book.

WE'RE IN THIS TOGETHER

The loss of a child is heartbreaking, complicated, and confusing. Your relationship with your child, their age, and the circumstances of their death will of course greatly impact your personal grief process. No two people are the same and therefore no two grief journeys will be either. This is a lonely trek you're on, but the path of child loss is well populated. There are many bereaved parents out there – more than any of us could imagine.

We're in this together. Though grief can be terribly lonely, no one should have to walk through the valley of loss alone. I hope this book becomes a kind, compassionate companion for you.

Be kind to yourself. Take your heart seriously.

Read on. May you find comfort in the pages ahead.

HOW CAN YOU BE GONE?

FROM THE GRIEVING HEART:

I don't know where to start.

I'm stunned, shocked, immobilized.

I've known you all your life. I held you right after you were born. I fed you, changed you, and watched you grow.

This can't be happening. How can you be gone?

How can I still be here, and you be gone? This is not possible. I'm supposed to go first. This is backwards and all wrong.

I don't know what to think or how to feel. It's like I've been hit by a truck. I'm dazed. Paralyzed.

My mind is spinning. I want to scream. I open my mouth, but nothing comes.

No, this cannot be.

My heart is in pieces. The world has changed.

Love is powerful. We're wired for connection and relationship. We're designed to love and be loved. The ties we have with our children are deep and powerful.

The loss of a child is difficult to understand, let alone experience. Unthinkable. Unbelievable. Backwards.

Our minds alternately spin and then freeze. Our hearts crack. Our bodies can be immobilized by the shock. We're stunned. We blink and wonder what happened, how, and why.

It feels as though the world has changed because it has. Our world has been altered forever. Our child – our beloved son or daughter - is missing.

Even if we've had other losses, this one is completely different. The loss of a child affects everything. It's as if all the oxygen has been sucked out of the atmosphere. We gasp and struggle to breathe.

Breathing seems to be all we can do at present. We breathe. Slowly. Deeply.

Affirmation: How can you be gone? I'm stunned. Dazed. I must breathe…

IS THIS WHAT A BROKEN HEART FEELS LIKE?

FROM THE GRIEVING HEART:

You're going to come through that door any moment.
You're going to text, call, or email any time now.

I just had a flashback of your tiny self, toddling
around the corner and smiling up at me.

You were just here. Where did you go?

How can this be?

I can feel the tears welling up inside. My thoughts are
bouncing all over the place. My heart is screaming.

I feel sick. My stomach is churning. I'm
lightheaded. The room is spinning.

Breathe. Yes, I must breathe.

Is this what a broken heart feels like?

This can't be real. You were just here. I swear I can hear your voice.

I'm closing my eyes. Please be there when I open them.

Please.

We're in this together. Our hearts are connected. We love passionately and deeply. Family ties run deep. Our attachment to our children is certainly one of our deepest human bonds.

We've known them all their lives. We watched them grow and develop. We grew up with them. We perhaps learned more from raising them than they learned from us.

When a child departs, there is a tearing that occurs. The separation of two objects glued firmly together is messy, and neither object is ever the same.

Love lasts. It endures. When a son or daughter dies, our hearts love on. They don't stop being our children and we don't cease to be their parents. We look for them. We listen for their voice. We keep expecting them to walk around the corner.

Then, reality hits. They're gone. We cry, sob, and even scream. The sudden intensity of grief can make us feel ill.

We grieve because we dared to love. Whether biological, adoptive, or step, the bond between a parent and a child is unique and powerful. This loss is shocking and unnerving. It hits us at the core of our being.

We let the tears flow. We let the sobs come. We scream if necessary. Our hearts are expressing our love through grief.

We will never be the same. How could we be? A tearing apart has occurred, and the pain is excruciating.

Affirmation: Because my love is deep, my grief will be intense. Tears are natural, and healthy.

HOW CAN THERE BE A WORLD WITHOUT YOU IN IT?

FROM THE GRIEVING HEART:

How can you be gone?

My heart is shocked, stunned, and broken. Perhaps shattered is a better word. I'm in pieces, all over the place.

And I'm sad. So sad.

You're gone, yet I act like you're still here. I wake up and expect you to be alive, just like you've always been.

How can there be a world without you in it?

Here come the tears again. I'm crying on the inside too. Tears everywhere. I'm one giant blob of sadness.

Your absence permeates everything. Everywhere I look, you're not there. And it hurts.

I feel nauseated.

Breathe. I must breathe. Breathe through the tears, through the sadness.

My heart is torn open. I'm spilling out all over everything.

This is awful.

I miss you.

Our heart is our most prized possession. It is the essence of who we are. When we love someone, our hearts are engaged. With our children, our hearts have been hyper-engaged since their birth or adoption.

At first, they were completely dependent on us. Their lives were literally in our hands. We weren't in control, of course. Anything could still have happened at any time. The parent-child bond is unique, intimate, and permanent.

When a parent-child love bond like this is severed by death, our hearts are torn. At first, we're stunned and in shock. Then we begin to feel the pain of loss.

We shake our heads in disbelief. Our minds struggle to grasp the unthinkable reality in front of us.

Our hearts begin to bleed emotion. A cloud of sadness descends upon us. We become hyper-aware of their absence. Out of habit and longing, we look for them, but to no avail. The reality that they are gone smacks us again and again and again.

Loss hurts. Our hearts have been sliced open. The pain is excruciating. The sadness is maddeningly intense.

How could we not be sad?

We keep breathing deeply. We give ourselves permission to be sad. We let the grief come. Our grief honors our child.

As our love is deep, so will our grief be.

Affirmation: I give myself permission to be sad. I will let the grief come.

HOW COULD THIS HAPPEN?

FROM THE GRIEVING HEART:

I woke up angry today.

I want you back. Now.

But you're not coming back, are you? No, of course not.

How could this happen? Why?

I don't understand.

I know we will all die someday, but kids aren't supposed to go before their parents. This is not right. This is backwards.

Why can't things stay the same? Why can't we all stay together, forever?

I don't like this anger, but sometimes it feels better than sadness. I find myself irritated with everything. My fuse is short. Frustration is bubbling just beneath the surface.

I think I'm going to explode. Maybe that would be better than holding this anger in. I don't know.

I want to scream and hit something. Maybe I should.

You're gone, and I'm angry.

When a child dies, our hearts break. Emotions pour out and flood our being. Sadness is one of the most common feelings we experience. Anger is another.

Our daughter or son is gone. We're stunned, shocked, and sad. We begin to feel the pain. Their absence becomes a cloud that encompasses us no matter where we go.

Questions begin to surface. How could this happen? Why? Why them? Why us? Why now? Why this way?

Satisfying answers are hard to come by. Even disease and accidents aren't sufficient reasons for their departure. We might understand what happened intellectually, but our hearts fidget with pent-up emotion. Anger begins to brew within.

Maybe we feel robbed and cheated. Perhaps we feel wronged or victimized. Our hearts rail against this loss, this death. We want them back. Now.

Love is passionate and powerful. It's as if our child was stolen from us. When we feel attacked, anger is a natural result.

Anger is common when we encounter the loss of a child. We love them. They're gone. Of course, we're upset – perhaps even livid. Loss has invaded and stolen part of our hearts. The key now is expressing the anger in healthy ways.

We could do any or all of the following:

- Hit a pillow or scream into it.
- Power walk around, punching the air.
- Knead some dough.
- Smack a punching bag.
- Write in a journal.
- Exercise.
- Vent to someone safe.

We can't afford to let the anger smolder and fester. It will most likely leak out in less than desirable ways. We must find ways to express it as it comes.

We continue to breathe deeply. We give ourselves permission to be angry. Anger is a natural part of grief.

Affirmation: It's okay if I get angry. I will find healthy ways to express my anger.

I COULDN'T PROTECT YOU

FROM THE GRIEVING HEART:

I have failed. I'm your parent. I should have protected you.

That's part of my job - protection. I swore to myself early on that I would take care of you and never let anything harm you. I would gladly lay down my own life to save yours.

I've protected you since you were born. Yes, some bad things happened to you. I blame myself for many of those too.

I thought those hurts and hardships were so big back then. I didn't have a clue. They were nothing. Nothing at all, compared to this.

But now this has happened. You're gone. I'm left here. I failed you.

I'm responsible for this. I didn't protect you.
I didn't act. I should have known.

I don't know what to do with this. The pain is excruciating. My thoughts torture me day and night.

I'm a sorry excuse for a parent. What parent can't protect their own child?

This can't be real. No. It just can't.

When our child came out of the womb, they were completely dependent on us. They could do nothing for themselves and relied on us for everything. They were so small and vulnerable. They were amazing, perfect little miracles. We held them and gazed at them in awe.

Our child. They were ours. Part of us. Even if they were adopted, our hearts attached and intertwined with theirs. Yes, this was meant to be.

Many of us were also semi-terrified. We were now responsible for this little life. We watched them all the time. We were hyper-aware and hyper-vigilant. We were constantly scanning for anything that could be a potential threat to this precious new life that had been entrusted to us.

Yes, they were entrusted to us. Our job was to provide everything they needed and to protect them from everything harmful. No matter how old our kids are, those original parental instincts are still active. All it takes is a need or a danger to activate them.

Now our child is gone. They have been taken from us - ripped from our watchful, loving arms. Something took them and we didn't stop it. We didn't protect them. We failed. Our hearts writhe in agony.

Of course, we logically know that we are not all-powerful and that we don't know everything. But as a parent, for the sake of our children, we expect ourselves to be both of these. When something bad or painful happens to our child, it's naturally our fault.

When pain or tragedy comes to our children, logic gives way to the heart. They are our children. We are their parents. We nurture, love, provide, and protect. Period.

No wonder we're devastated. Not only is our child gone, but we're to blame. The guilt can be stifling. The emotional pain is more than words can possibly describe.

We must take our hearts seriously. We must begin to process this powerful sense of guilt and responsibility for what happened. We couldn't protect them, and our hearts must feel their way through this. We must find healthy ways to express this festering guilt and get it out.

We breathe deeply. In through the nose, and out through the mouth. Over and over. We express what's happening inside us. We talk, write, and share. As we give our hearts the space they need to grieve and mourn, we will see things more clearly over time.

Affirmation: I didn't protect you. Perhaps I couldn't. That's hard to swallow. Protection has been my job for so long. I'll let my heart feel this pain. You're worth mourning for.

FOR REFLECTION AND/OR JOURNALING

MY GRIEVING HEART:

"If I were to make a list of words describing how I've felt since losing you, I would say…"

EVERYTHING FEELS DIFFERENT NOW

FROM THE GRIEVING HEART:

I feel confused.

One minute I'm sad, and the next I'm angry. I zone out and find myself staring at the walls. Everything seems strange, like I'm in some alternate reality that looks a lot like my old life.

This isn't my old life. You're not here.

My life is not the same at all. Everything feels different now.

Then the sadness returns. Or maybe it never left. Perhaps sadness is more like a cloud that follows me throughout the day.

My emotions are all over the place, and I'm getting less able to manage and hide them. I feel unstable. I'm not acting like myself. I feel different.

The world around me marches on like nothing happened, while I'm stuck here. It's like I've become an observer – an outsider looking in.

I look for you everywhere, all the time.

I miss you. I want my old life back.

What is life now? I'm confused.

When we lose a child, our hearts crack, and emotion pours out everywhere. Some parents manage to hide some of their feelings, only to find them leaking out here and there in unhealthy ways. Some express their emotions freely but in such a way that is not helpful to them. Others learn ways of managing grief emotions that express who they are and their relationship with their children.

If our children were older and our relationship with them was on-and-off, challenging, or complicated, this might add to the emotional upheaval we experience.

When this unruly combo of sadness, anger, anxiety, fear, guilt, and frustration hits, confusion naturally occurs. We've never been here before, even if we've previously lost another child. Every parent-child relationship is unique, and so is every loss. This is unchartered territory.

No matter what we thought it might be like, the terrain we find ourselves in is different than we imagined or expected. Nothing could have fully prepared us for this.

Our minds are trying to somehow make sense of what happened and this new reality that has been thrust upon us. Our hearts are reeling from the collision of life and loss. Our daughter or son has died and left a massive void. There are gaping holes in our hearts and in our routines. Some confusion is common and expected.

Learning to be patient with ourselves is important. The path is rocky, uneven, and unpredictable. Grief is more like a marathon than a sprint. Pacing ourselves along the way is more crucial than we realize.

We're not superhuman. We can breathe deeply and give ourselves permission to not have to understand all the events unfolding in our lives or be able to explain them to others.

Life is anything but business as usual right now. Everything has changed.

Affirmation: Loss is confusing. I'll be patient with myself.

CHILDREN ARE EVERYWHERE

FROM THE GRIEVING HEART:

I see other families out there. It hurts.

I see parents and children together smiling and laughing. Holding hands and skipping. Talking and playing. My heart breaks - again and again.

It seems like my heart has broken so many times that soon nothing will be left. I feel like I'm barely here as it is.

All I can think about is you.

I resent the carefree happiness of others. Just the sight of a happy child crushes me.

The world is closing in on me. I can't get enough air. I feel claustrophobic. Danger and emotional pain seem to be everywhere. My heart is disintegrating, bit by bit.

If I can't stand to see other families, where does that leave me? They're everywhere. Next door. Down the street. In supermarkets and stores. In restaurants and movie theaters. On billboards and in advertisements.

As I drive along, it's like I can feel the presence of other children in the houses along the roads. I can see them riding bikes and walking on the sidewalks, even if there's no one there. I pass schools every day.

All the world is a reminder that you're gone. I look for you everywhere. I miss you.

I hate seeing other families right now. I hate that I hate seeing happy children. Who am I? What am I becoming?

Awful. This is truly awful.

After the loss of a child, just seeing other children and families can be excruciatingly painful. Every visual of a child - or a child and a parent - stabs our hearts, and the grief comes tumbling out. It's as if our hearts are a mass of painful wounds and bruises waiting to be bumped and punched by life.

Feeling sad, angry, and even confused by seeing other children and families is natural and common for a parent enduring the death of a child. Our precious son or daughter has been taken from us, and we're reeling with the shock. We're stunned and paralyzed. Our hearts are like shattered glass strewn all over the place. Nothing is the same.

We see another child and our hearts scream with pain and longing. How could this happen? Why? Why our child? Why now? Why this way? Why us?

Unfair. Backwards. Wrong. We shake our heads. No, this can't be. Such things should not happen. Logically, we know such unthinkable tragedies do happen - every day. But not to us. Not to our child.

This pain is unique. There is nothing else like it. No other loss we have endured or could ever face comes close. This is deep, personal, and pervasive. This was our child. Ours.

Some days, just getting out of bed might take massive effort. Every step into the world can feel emotionally dangerous. We're feeling our loss. This death has overtaken us and permeated everything. Right now, the loss of our child has become the lens through which we see everything.

We must give ourselves permission to hurt - to be sad, angry, confused, and all the rest. All the emotions and all the pain honor our child. Our grief proclaims our love. The intensity of our mourning shouts how unique and special they were and are to us.

This is unknown territory for us. Everything might look the same, but it's not. The world has changed, forever. Each step is new. We must be patient with ourselves, breathe deeply, and do what we know to take care of ourselves today. Our child would want that.

Affirmation: Seeing other children and parents might be painful for me. I'll use the pain to help me grieve and express my love for you. My heart is broken, and I miss you desperately.

I SHOULD HAVE GONE FIRST

FROM THE GRIEVING HEART:

"No one should have to bury their children."

How many times have I heard that? I agree. But now I'm living it. It's all wrong somehow.

I should have gone first. That's the way it works. Parents have children. Parents raise children. Parents release their kids into the world. Parents keep being parents — until the parents die. The baton gets passed and the kids live on.

This is the natural order of things. This - what I'm experiencing - is not natural. It's backward. Reversed. Wrong.

Wrong. I keep coming back to that word. I find myself saying, "This is all wrong," again and again.

It should have been me. You should be here. I should be gone.

I know I'm going in circles with this. It's a loop I can't seem to break out of. Maybe I'm just in denial. I don't want this to be real. My heart refuses to accept it. My mind can't even grasp it, so what chance does my heart have in this?

What parent should ever have to say the ultimate goodbye to their child?

Wrong. It's all wrong.

There is a natural order to things that most of us take for granted after a while. Certain things are expected and anticipated. Other things are out of the ordinary but are common enough to be accepted. Still other things seem unnatural, unfair, out of place, and devastating. Our hearts scream that such things should never happen.

The loss of a child is one of the latter.

People are born, live their lives, and then pass on. That's what we see as the natural order. Grandparents pass on first, then parents, and then the children, and so on. When this expected timeline is interrupted, it's as if time stops and begins moving backwards. Life feels reversed, upended. Something is amiss. It feels wrong.

We're designed for relationship. Our connection with our kids is powerful, even mysterious. Most would say there's something deeply spiritual about it. Separation from our children - especially via death - is not something we anticipate, plan on, or even care to contemplate.

Children should not die. Period. So, when death comes knocking, it's a foreign invader whose time schedule is off. It's unexpected, unwanted, and terrifying. When it's our child involved, death doesn't merely knock, but barges in and trashes everything. When we come to, our child is gone, and we're left wondering how this happened and why.

Of course, we know intellectually that the natural order of things gets frequently upended. Life does not work as we anticipate or as we think it's supposed to. But the death of a child hits the heart in ways that nothing else does. This is the one part of the natural order that should never be violated.

But here we are. We're still here, and our child is gone. We're enduring the unthinkable. We buried our children. We attended their funerals. Now, our hearts beat differently. We wake up every day in a different world.

Today, we breathe deeply. We take things one step at a time. We give ourselves permission to grieve. We let our hearts feel and process the unthinkable.

Affirmation: Losing you feels all wrong. This is not what I anticipated or expected. I'll take my heart seriously today and take one step at a time.

I WISH MONEY WASN'T SUCH A BIG DEAL

FROM THE GRIEVING HEART:

I wish money wasn't such a big deal. It can be such a pain — and so stressful.

Bills keep coming. There are more expenses than I could have imagined. Losing you was enough. I don't want to have to worry about money, too.

Just having to think about finances right now is frustrating - even infuriating. There are too many decisions to make. A new decision pops up every day, if not every hour.

I miss you and want to grieve. Frankly, I could care less about money. And yet, I'm worried about it too.

I resent all these decisions that must be made. I'm drowning in paperwork and details.

Life moves right on as if nothing happened. My world, however, has stopped. You're not here.

I'm angry, sad, and frustrated.

Can't the world be a little kinder and slow down for a while?

Financial management can be stressful even in settled seasons of our lives. Depending on the situation, when a child departs, money issues can descend upon us from every direction. Like ocean waves, things to do and decisions that must be made keep rolling in. Our already broken hearts can feel further battered and bruised.

Bills. Phone calls. Death certificates. Banks. Investments. The list goes on and on.

We can feel violated. We're stunned. We're grieving and the emotions can be intense. These details - which we know are important and can't be ignored - invade and chip away at us. Decisions relentlessly poke and prod our already battered souls. Our minds reel under the weight of a to-do list we didn't want or ask for.

Depending on our circumstances, it might seem that the entire world is looking for a yes, a no, a signature, or an action of some kind. And the monetary issues we needed an answer about yesterday seem to all come with a large label that says, "Wait."

Though frustrating, these financial matters are part of our grief journey. Let the emotions come. We must find healthy ways to express them - talking out loud, writing in a journal, sharing with others, etc. We need some helpful, healthy people who can walk with us through this.

We grieve one step, one moment at a time.

Affirmation: Money and financial matters can be frustrating and draining. I'll handle them one at a time.

I FEEL LIKE I'M GOING IN CIRCLES

FROM THE GRIEVING HEART:

I miss you. Badly.

I'm glad I have videos. I find myself watching them over and over. I close my eyes and listen to your voice. What a wonderful, sweet voice you had.

I open my eyes and expect to see you. I can't believe you're gone.

How did this happen? Why? Why you?

I keep asking the same questions. My mind runs around the same track, again and again. I feel like I'm going in circles.

And yet, I'm going nowhere. I'm barely moving at all. I go from thing to thing, person to person, without seeing anything. I'm a shadow, flitting in and out of what the rest of the world calls "normal life."

What's normal now? Everything has changed. I don't like this world anymore because you're not in it.

Can you hear me? Where are you?

I look around. It seems like the same world, but it's not. Far from it.

I'm a ball of emotion. Sad. Angry. Frustrated. Confused. Sometimes it's hard to tell one emotion from another. I feel hijacked, like I've been kidnapped and taken to some alternate reality.

Surreal. That's the word I was looking for.

Our child is gone. Our hearts are broken. We've taken an unthinkable, massive hit, and our minds are in survival mode. Even if this death was expected, our hearts could never be fully prepared for our son or daughter to take their last breath.

Our souls grapple to understand this new reality of a world without our child. We will always deny what we are not prepared to accept, and we're certainly not ready to accept life without them yet.

Even though they're gone, their place in our hearts remains secure. We look for them. We listen for their voice. We try to keep them close any way we can. Pictures. Videos. Texts. Voicemails. Letters. Our search is part of love in action.

Each morning we expect to wake in the same world as yesterday. This illusion is now shattered. We live in a different place now — one without our child. Everything seems off, strange, weird.

Life is surreal.

Navigating all these emotions and changes seems about as doable as a solo swim of the Pacific. This is no longer the same world. Not for us. We did not ask for or want this change. Loss invaded, and then grief moved in. Our child's departure is shaking our universe.

Our minds will spin. Emotions will hijack us. Our hearts will ask repetitive questions. Our souls will search for answers. We are feeling our child's absence.

Affirmation: Life is surreal. I'm trying to make sense of things. This will take time.

FOR REFLECTION AND/OR JOURNALING

MY GRIEVING HEART:

"At present, what I'm finding most challenging in this grief process is..."

I WAS ONE OF YOUR FIRST BEST FRIENDS

FROM THE GRIEVING HEART:

Your world was so small at first. We held you, nurtured you, adored you. You were the center of our universe.

You looked at us and smiled. I can still hear your infant laughter. Delightful. Amazing.

Memories and mental pictures flit in and out of my mind. Your little hands and feet. Your first steps. Your first words. Your first everything.

In many ways, I guess I was one of your first best friends. You didn't have any friends yet, and we were everything to you.

And you were everything to us.

More memories. How we laughed and played together. Where we went and the things we did. The funny and wonderful things you said and did.

You were a little miracle. You still are.

I'm smiling right now. It feels good to smile. You mean so much to me. How can you be gone?

I know this is real, but I cannot accept this yet. I don't want to. I will never want to. I don't want this to be happening.

I want you back, here, now.

I am still your first best friend. I will always be your parent.

In many ways, we were our child's first best friend. We were with them almost all the time. We laughed and smiled as they turned over, babbled, said their first words, and learned to pull themselves up. When they took their first steps, we reacted like the most amazing thing in history had just taken place.

They trusted us. We loved and adored them. They picked up our words and mannerisms. They became little reflections of us. They felt safe and secure when we were in the room.

Yes, we were their first best friends. We were their world, and they were ours. We weren't perfect parents, but we were theirs.

Some of us may have come from less than ideal home environments. Our backgrounds may have been complicated, confusing, and painful. When our child was born, we never dreamed we could love anything or anyone like this. We decided to be the best parents possible – the best parents ever.

After all, our son or daughter deserved the very best.

Though no one is perfect, we thought our child was close. They could do no wrong. They were ours, and we were theirs. Life was full of joy and expectation.

Times were so innocent then. Life was about the basics. Love. Care. Nurture. Family.

These things now come flooding back. Memories swarm around us. We remember what was. We want our child back, now.

Affirmation: You were my everything, and I was your world. Being your parent is such an honor. I love you.

THERE'S SO MUCH I DON'T UNDERSTAND

FROM THE GRIEVING HEART:

Last night, I dreamed of you. We were walking through a meadow. A gentle breeze was blowing. There were mountains in front of us.

At first, we were side by side. You held my hand, just like you did when you were little. After a while, you began walking a little ahead of me. We walked down a hill and arrived at a peaceful stream. It was so beautiful.

You walked into the water and then turned and looked at me. You smiled, and I could see the love in your eyes. Then you turned around and waded back in.

I tried to follow, but I couldn't move. I panicked. I called out to you, but you kept going. As you got closer to the other side, you began to slowly disappear. Then you were gone.

When I woke up, I could feel the tears streaming down my face.

What was that? What does it mean?

Are you telling me you're okay? Was that a goodbye of some kind? Did I just get a little glimpse of heaven?

I was glad to see you, if only in a dream.

Somehow, you feel less far away today. I know you're gone. And yet, I still have you somehow.

There's so much I don't understand.

Our child is always on our minds. It's not surprising, therefore, if they appear in our dreams.

It's been said that we heal while we sleep. Our bodies rest and rejuvenate. Our minds often grapple with what we can't consciously process during the day. Dreams can be an attempt to reconnect with our child and to somehow make more sense of what happened.

Not everyone has dreams of their child, and not every dream is a positive or reassuring one.

Our minds don't rest well after this loss. Our worlds are shaken, and our sleep is naturally affected. If dreams of our child come, we naturally want to know what they mean. In most cases, the best place to look for an interpretation is our own hearts.

When we have dreams of our daughter or son, it is certainly related intimately to our grief process.

Some dreams might generate more questions. Others might reassure us and bring more peace to our hearts. Still others might stir or intensify our longings.

We continue to practice breathing deeply. We will be patient with ourselves on this unpredictable journey. What we don't understand now might make more sense later.

We should consider what our heart is telling us and grieve as well as we know how at this point in our journey. Our grief honors our child.

Affirmation: There are many things I won't understand. I'll be patient with myself.

NOTHING COULD HAVE PREPARED ME FOR THIS

FROM THE GRIEVING HEART:

I don't know how to do this.

I remember thinking once, when someone I knew lost a child, what I would do if I lost you.

I drove the thought from my mind. Ridiculous. Impossible. That wasn't going to happen. Not to you. Not to us.

Now, here I am. You're gone. Nothing could have prepared me for this.

I miss you. I want to see you and hear your voice. I want to touch you.

I love you.

Even if I wasn't with you, I've been here for your every breath. And I'm still here. How could you, my child, come and go and I'm still here.

This doesn't make sense. Nothing makes sense.

I can't imagine life without you, even though that's the life I'm living now. I keep expecting you to come around the corner, to text, or to call.

I feel terrible. I'm sad. I feel alone. Everyone's looking at me, like they're trying to size up how I'm doing. People I counted on have disappeared. I guess they don't know what to do with this either.

Why did you have to go? My heart keeps trying to find a way to reverse history and make you reappear somehow. I can't let you go. I'm not ready. I don't know think I'll ever be ready.

I love you. I miss you.

We miss them. Deeply. The longing within us can be painful.

The love of a parent for a child is powerful, deep, mysterious, and spiritual. For many, it begins the moment of conception and grows with each passing moment. For adoptive parents, it often begins before we are even aware of their existence or see the first picture.

The love of a mom or dad for a child is unique, special, and permanent. It will not be dislodged or evicted. Though our relationship with our kids changes as they grow, they will always be our children. And we will always be their parents.

Love remains. It plows through every obstacle. It finds a way over every barrier. It battles every threat. It winces with every conflict, separation, or estrangement. Love is the fuel that drives our parental engines.

Love endures all things. It knows no time limit.

Our children are a part of us. Life and love have carved a permanent place for them in our hearts and lives. Their physical presence may be gone, yet everything about them lingers around us. Their smile, laughter, words, actions, and influence remain, hovering around us, bouncing about in our minds.

Memories have become painful and wonderful at the same time.

When this loss strikes the heart, we naturally withdraw a little. Stunned, we need time to collect ourselves and begin to tussle with the unwanted and the unthinkable. We're not ourselves at present. Our family and friends notice this and often don't know what to do with it.

We feel alone. Grief is naturally a lonely process, even if we're surrounded by people. We can feel alone in a crowd of people who care about us.

We miss our child. We will continue loving and missing them. We look for them. We listen for their voice. We long for them. Their absence will stun us again and again.

We love them. Our grief proclaims our love.

Affirmation: I'm missing you. Feeling alone is natural when grieving. I'll remember that my grief proclaims my love for you.

I NEVER KNEW LITTLE THINGS COULD BE SO HEAVY

FROM THE GRIEVING HEART:

Details are strangling me.

Everywhere I look there's something to be done. Life is normally full of stuff to do, but your death has sent things over the top.

I stare at my list. I resent it. I don't want this to be real. I know these things must be done, but I can feel my heart's resistance.

I go in circles about what decisions need to be made. What about this? What about that? I feel paralyzed. All I want is you back.

Then I feel guilty for procrastinating. I get up the next day, and of course the list is still there. Maybe I think that if I ignore it enough it will eventually disappear.

Details. Stuff. I never knew little things could add up to be this heavy.

I feel like I need wisdom I don't have. I need discipline I don't have energy for.

The void you've left is immense. The emptiness is intense. Even when I'm surrounded by people, I feel adrift, alone in a lifeboat in the middle of the ocean.

My heart just wants all this to go away and for you to come back.

I want life as it was. I want you.

Our personal worlds have ground to a halt. The unthinkable has happened. We're dazed, paralyzed. We stare in disbelief as the world around us continues to speed onward. Responsibilities and details come knocking.

Details can wear us down. They come at us every day. They swirl around in our minds and disturb us in the middle of the night. Perhaps we even wake panicked and terrorized. The future and our to-do list can loom over us like a dark, forbidding storm cloud.

We wonder what's next. Perhaps we're internally bracing for the next disaster.

A demanding to-do list of details can set off a different sort of grief storm. We can feel annoyed and angry about all that needs to be done. Responsibilities or to-do items related specifically to our child are packed full of foreboding and dread. We don't want to be doing this. We want our child back – now. Certain things on our list wave our loss in our faces. The grief smacks us again and again.

Having to handle all the details and responsibilities of life naturally stirs our emotions. We don't want to be doing this. Our hearts need freedom to process, feel, and grieve. The oxygen has been sucked out of our lives and we're having trouble breathing.

Routine responsibilities and extraneous details can feel like an irreverent intrusion at a sacred time.

We might be in the equivalent of the Grief ICU - broken, bruised, semi-paralyzed, and in pain. And yet, we have all these decisions and responsibilities coming at us. Imagine a group of people crowded around a bed in an ICU unit screaming questions and waving papers (all at the same time) at a barely conscious patient. Ridiculous.

And yet, that's what it feels like to many of us.

Our hearts need space. Lots of space. The world around us screams its urgent demands. We must breathe deeply and look to our own hearts. What's most important? What can we handle next that's realistic and doable? We'll do that, and then see.

One thing at a time. One moment at a time.

Affirmation: My heart is my most important possession. I'll take care of it today. I'll handle what I can, as I can.

I CAN HEAR YOU CALLING

FROM THE GRIEVING HEART:

I woke up in the middle of the night. I could hear you calling me.

Maybe I was dreaming, but it seemed so real. I've heard that call many times. I jumped up and started to head for your room. Then I realized I wasn't in the same house anymore - that you weren't here anymore. I slumped back onto the bed and buried my head in my hands.

Losing you is torture. My mind can't seem to let go. My heart won't and probably never will. We're connected, so how does this separation thing work?

How many times did you call me, and I didn't hear you? How many times did you need me, and I wasn't there?

I wish I could hear your voice. It was good to hear you in my dream, or whatever it was. And you were calling me. That's special. You're special.

If I close my eyes, I can almost hear you calling me now. It's like you live somewhere inside me. I hear you in my heart.

My heart is broken over losing you, my child. There was no one like you. One of a kind. Unique. Priceless. You were mine, and I was yours.

How did this happen? What do I do with this?

Our child's voice is special. We've heard it so many times that it has taken up residence in our hearts. It echoes inside us. We think we hear them calling.

Our job as parents is to love and meet our child's needs. When a child dies, our hearts naturally wonder what we could have done to prevent this. Was there a need we didn't meet? Did they call and we didn't hear them? What did we miss?

The incessant internal questioning can be torturous. Our minds spin. Our broken hearts desperately cling to our child in any way we can.

There is such deep connection in the parent-child bond. There is no other relationship like it. Our child is a part of us. Now they're gone. What does that mean? How can we survive this?

We need to talk. We need to say their name and share our memories. We need to air our questions, frustrations, and confusion. We need to get what's happening inside us out somehow.

We need people who are trustworthy and accepting to listen and be with us in this. We don't need fixes. There are none. We don't need advice we haven't asked for. We need open hearts and listening ears to exist with us in this turmoil, if only for a little while.

When we're hurt, we tend to isolate. Our hearts warn us that this is not the thing to do. We're relational creatures. Our response to this loss proves that. We need solid, loving relationships right now. Where do we find them?

Perhaps we already have them? Maybe these people have yet to show up in our lives. We look around us. We trust that the safe souls we need are out there. On the one hand, we trust they will appear at the right time. On the other hand, we search for them.

Our hearts matter. We can't afford to go this alone.

Affirmation: Even though I'm hurting, I can't afford to isolate. I trust that the people I need to walk with me in this are out there. I will find ways to express this grief, as best I can.

FOR REFLECTION AND/OR JOURNALING

MY GRIEVING HEART:

"When I think about you and all that's happened, I still have questions. Like...."

I FEEL EMPTY

FROM THE GRIEVING HEART:

I woke up today and felt numb. I was just there. I didn't feel anything at all.

I stared at the ceiling. I lost all sense of time. I got up and went through the motions, hating every step.

I thought my heart was broken. Now I'm wondering if it has departed altogether. I'm a shell. I feel empty.

Your absence is everywhere.

Sometimes I get a little relief. Then something will bring you to mind, and I feel guilty for having forgotten you, even for a moment.

Your absence has spread and now permeates my existence. You're not here. You're not there. You're not anywhere I'm going to be today. The rest of my life will be spent without you.

The thought of that is more than I can bear.

I'm numb, but at the same time angry. Don't ask me to explain that. I can't.

I don't know much of anything right now, except that I miss you.

I still can't believe you're gone. I can't accept this.

I won't accept it. Ever.

The heart can only handle so much. Broken and even shattered, we need breaks from the constant, grinding pressure of grief and its emotions.

With the loss of a child, our hearts shift into survival mode. Eventually, our feelers shut down. We stare at walls, ceilings, and people. We look but cease to see. Life flows on, but we are not a part of it. The sadness, anger, frustration, confusion, guilt, and anxiety all add up, and the heart powers down. We feel empty, listless, even lifeless.

The loss of a child changes everything. It's all too much. It can feel like our hearts have departed.

We grow numb.

We move in and out of this numb place. The heart takes a break and then begins to feel again. When the emotion gets too intense, it takes another brief hiatus. Like an electrical breaker being tripped or the emergency stop at a gas station being pushed, we momentarily switch off.

This on-and-off life is exhausting. Life is anything but "normal." In fact, nothing quite feels, looks, or even tastes the same. Grief is pounding our entire system. Our child's absence colors everything.

We practice breathing deeply and slowly. We give ourselves permission to be emotional, confused, and numb. We take our hearts seriously. We practice being patient with ourselves. We can power down when we need to. Overall, we learn to expect less of ourselves.

Grief is squeezing our minds, hearts, and bodies. The only way to deal with grief is to grieve.

Affirmation: I may feel numb at times. That's okay.
My heart is working to manage the unmanageable.

EVERYONE WANTS ME TO FEEL BETTER

FROM THE GRIEVING HEART:

I feel like a robot. I'm going through the motions. I don't want to go anywhere or do anything. Why can't life just stop for a while?

This is unfair. Even cruel. Everyone expects me to go on as usual, as if I'm doing great and the same person I was before you left.

Ridiculous. I'm not the same. How could I be? If I just went on as before, what would that say about you?

You're my child, whether you're here or not. I love you. I miss you. I'm not the same. I'll never be the same again.

Why can't the world accept that? Why can't my own friends and family accept that?

Everyone wants me to feel better. No one wants me to be hurting. But how realistic is that? Expecting me to be "fine" is like expecting a head-on collision to have no effect whatsoever on the cars or people involved.

Little children aren't supposed to die. Adult children aren't supposed to die before their parents. This is all wrong somehow. You should be here.

I want you here, now.

Yes, this is ridiculous.

She is still our daughter. He is still our son. We are still their parents. We didn't stop loving them, and we never will.

There is much about loss and grief which makes logical sense, but emotionally our hearts have trouble grappling with it. We're wired for relationship and built for connection. Over time, our lives become a web of relationships. When one strand is severed, our entire life-web reverberates with the shock.

Our children are special, unique, and powerful strands of our web. They came from us. They're a part of us. Their strands are connected to ours in mysteriously deep and intimate ways. When a child dies and this strand is broken, it feels like our own life is pouring out into the emptiness left by their departure.

Much like breaking a leg, we become instantly focused on the pain and its source. What once was simple, like walking, has become excruciatingly painful and almost impossible. Routine, everyday life immediately changes into a set of Mount Everest-like challenges.

The rest of the world seems unchanged. Others' webs have not been struck, and their lives move along as usual. It feels like we've been transported to another planet and are being forced to live a different life trying to navigate unruly emotions and unrealistic expectations. And it feels like we're doing it alone.

Ridiculous. Yes, that's a good word for it.

There may be times we might feel like robots. We go through the motions, doing our best to stay functional. There is so much going on inside us, far more than we can understand, feel, or manage all at once.

As much as possible, we take one moment, one step at a time. We let the grief be what it is. We try to accept ourselves as we are, in this moment.

Affirmation: I'll work on accepting myself while grieving, one moment, one step at a time.

I'M NOT WHO I WAS

FROM THE GRIEVING HEART:

Where have my friends gone?

They were compassionate for a while, but now I sense they're avoiding me. They don't call, text, or email.

I sense I don't fit in anymore. Something has happened. Losing you is changing me. I'm not who I was.

When I do see them, it's awkward. They don't know what to say or do. It's uncomfortable, weird, and lonely.

And they never mention you.

Sometimes it feels like I've got an infectious disease. Better not get too close to me. Maybe I should wear a sign.

I'm mad. Frustrated. Confused. Hurt. First, I lost you. That was devastating enough. Now, it feels like I'm losing others too.

I hate this. I want it all to go away. I want you back.

I miss you.

When we lose a child, our entire relational network is affected. One of the thickest strands of our life web has been severed and now all the other strands are trembling.

This is natural, and even inevitable in many cases. But it is also frustrating, confusing, and extremely painful.

We can feel forsaken, abandoned, and rejected by our friends and even family members. If we come from a difficult, traumatic, or abusive past, our past pain can be surfaced by these current losses. We're thrust into a new world that looks the same, but where everything is different. All the rules have changed. Emotionally, we're treading water, desperately trying to stay afloat somehow.

Our child is gone. Our foundation is now cracked. We can feel like the earth beneath our feet has vanished and we have no solid ground to stand on.

Feeling invisible or even shunned on top of this heartbreaking loss seems unfair and even cruel. The pain can strike deep and plant seeds of bitterness inside us. Our hearts can't afford this.

We must find ways to forgive quickly. We must release the unhelpful statements and actions of others as they occur. We must guard our hearts from being infiltrated by these harmful viruses.

Our worlds are different now. Everything has changed. We're in pain. This will not be fixed. We've lost our child.

Affirmation: All my relationships seem to be changing. I don't like this. I will hold all things loosely, forgive quickly, and grieve as best as I know how.

AM I GOING CRAZY?

FROM THE GRIEVING HEART:

I'm forgetting things.

Appointments. Where I put my car keys.
What I came into the room for.

I'm losing words. I have trouble talking in complete sentences and making sense sometimes. I blip out in the middle of conversations, and when I come back to reality, I'm confronted by blank stares and even laughter.

I'm not myself. How could I be myself? You're not here anymore.

This is frustrating and embarrassing. It's as if part of me is fading away.

You're a massive part of me. If you're no longer here, what does that mean for me?

I feel strange.

Some people are worried about me. Others are starting to give me this, "Come on! Get over it!" look.

Maybe they're right. Perhaps your death has damaged me somehow. Maybe I'm the problem. Am I going crazy?

When you left, maybe my sanity departed too.

Losing a child is traumatic. It hits every part of our being and our life. Grief squeezes us, and sometimes there is not much left over for living "normal" or "routine" life.

In fact, normal, as we knew it, is gone.

Just as our hearts have been hit, our minds are taking a beating too. Grief and the corresponding emotions are taking up more space and requiring a vast amount of focus and energy. We can find that our mental capacity may be naturally challenged and even reduced for a time.

Forgetfulness begins to show itself. Memory issues surface. We blank out, even in the middle of important conversations. We can't seem to pull up what we knew yesterday. We can't remember where we were this morning or where we're supposed to be next.

In an age when we're on the alert for mental illness, dementia, and Alzheimer's, this is scary. We naturally wonder what's happening to us. Are we going crazy?

No. We're not crazy, but we are in a crazy-making situation. We've lost a child. Life's usual borders are being strained. Intense and deep grief has been added to our lives on top of all that we do and are responsible for. The pressure can be immense. It can wear us down.

We will most likely notice a change in our mental capacity for a while. Our system is on overload, so it naturally eliminates items our hearts don't see as necessary to our survival.

We are not the same. Everything is affected right now, including our minds.

We're not crazy but accepting that we're not at our best is important. We can give ourselves a break. All our margin is being gobbled up by grief. This is natural and normal.

Affirmation: I feel crazy sometimes because losing you is insane.
I will learn to accept that I'm not at my mental best right now.

I'M NOT SLEEPING WELL

FROM THE GRIEVING HEART:

I'm not sleeping well.

I have trouble getting to sleep. I toss and turn. I can't seem to get comfortable. My mind races.

And inevitably, lying there in the dark, I find myself thinking about you. That doesn't help, but I can't drive you from my brain. I don't want to. I want to remember. But I want to sleep too.

Sometimes I lie there for hours. Other nights I cry myself to sleep. If I read, that seems to help.

I wake up a lot. I have dreams. I'm looking for you even in my sleep. Some nights I wake anxious or even panicky. When morning finally arrives, I'm anything but refreshed.

I walk around in a daze. I'm tired all the time. I end up drifting off at work. I get drowsy in the car. This is not good.

What do I do with this? Do I need help?

I keep hoping this will get better, but it goes on night after night. Even if I do sleep one night, there's no guarantee about the next. I'm starting to get anxious about this, and I dread nighttime.

You are always on my mind. I still can't believe this. How could you be gone?

For restful sleep to occur, most of us need a sense of normalcy and safety.

With the loss of a child, normalcy disappears, and our personal sense of safety and well-being can be shaken. The emotions are intense. Sleep disturbances are a natural result.

Life has completely changed. Nothing is the same, including our sleep. When we lie down and the distractions fade, thoughts that we've been keeping at bay drift back into our consciousness. Our minds begin to race. We think about life as it was. We dwell on what happened, when, how, and why. We ask the numerous unanswerable questions and ruminate on them, over and over. We imagine what we could have done, if we had only known. Though it's time to wind down, our emotions may be gearing up.

Our child's absence is palpable. Falling asleep becomes difficult. Staying asleep becomes a challenge. Even if we sleep, resting peacefully and waking refreshed is not the norm in heavy grief.

It has been said that sleep deprivation is the most basic form of torture. Given the fact that grief isn't a quick journey, it's not surprising that we feel cranky, irritable, sad, anxious, or depressed. With sleep patterns altered, no wonder work performance and relationships are more of a challenge.

Letting our doctor know what's happening and what we're going through is important. There is no shame in seeking some help to get good sleep and pursue better health during this time. There are many options, both medical and natural. We should consult someone we trust. What has been helpful to others who have lost children? What seems to fit best with who we are and our situation? What can we do to get more of the rest that we need?

Sleep disturbances in grief are common. We can be patient with ourselves and take the next step toward taking good care of ourselves during this time.

Affirmation: My life has been upended, so it makes sense my sleep would be disrupted. I'll focus on loving you by grieving well and trust this will change over time.

FOR REFLECTION AND/OR JOURNALING

MY GRIEVING HEART:

"If I were to list some of what's different since losing you, I would say..."

I THOUGHT I WAS A LITTLE BETTER

FROM THE GRIEVING HEART:

I thought I was a little better, but I guess not.

I was doing fine, having a good day, until I heard that song. It took me back. Thoughts of you came flooding in. I was a basket case in a nanosecond.

I never know what's going to happen next. The grief is always there, slowly building up inside me. It grows until my system is full, and then along comes a person, place, aroma, word, or song that reminds me of you.

A switch gets flipped. A hatch pops open, and all the pressurized emotion comes bursting out. I have no control over when, where, or how.

This is frustrating and embarrassing. I take one step forward, and then two steps back. The grief seems to be getting deeper. The more I grieve, the more the grief inside me seems to grow.

It all seems so backward. How do I know if I'm making progress? Is progress what I should even be thinking about? What does "good" grieving look like?

I find one answer, then generate two more questions. Is grief some never-ending cycle? Will I ever feel better? Do I want to feel better?

If feeling better means I stop thinking about you, then forget it. I'll hold onto you, any way I can.

I've lost you, and yet I fear losing you. This is all so strange and confusing.

Grief is a dynamic process. It's always moving. It's highly individual, defies prediction, and refuses to be boxed in. It's all a bit mysterious. It's a matter of the heart.

After the loss of a child, each day is a journey through a virtual minefield. We never know where the next grief burst is hiding. Anything can trigger it. The heart is looking for ways to express itself and to declare its love. We bump into unseen memories suddenly and without warning. Reminders of our child are everywhere.

The heart is trying to find a way to live with our child's absence. The connections are mysterious, powerful, and deep. We're thinking of and looking for them, even when we're not aware of it. Loss has invaded our lives and is demanding our attention.

One day we feel we're doing well. The next day might not be so smooth. One moment might be great, and the next we might be showering the sidewalk with tears. One minute, we're fine, and the next we're struggling to keep intense emotions in check.

Welcome to the grief roller coaster. It's full of ups, downs, and sudden twists. It yanks and jerks us here and there, leaving us gasping for breath. It's never smooth for long. And it's not over in 90 seconds either. It goes on, and on, and on.

This isn't a roller coaster we chose to get on. We simply woke up one day and discovered we were passengers. What's important now is making sure our seat belts are fastened, keeping our arms and legs in the car, and riding this whirling, curling monster as well as possible.

It's hard to measure our own progress on this grief journey. There will be ups and downs, and some will be breathtaking. Some turns we will see coming, while others will take us completely by surprise. We simply grieve as best we can from moment to moment. We take life as it comes, one step at a time.

When the grief surges up and spews out, so be it. Every grief burst honors our child and declares our love for them.

Affirmation: My grief declares my love for you. I'll ride this grief roller-coaster as best I can, one moment at a time.

WHERE DID EVERYONE GO?

FROM THE GRIEVING HEART:

This would be easier if it weren't for the people around me. At least, that's the way it feels.

Right after you left, people were everywhere. Tears. Hugs. Offers of support poured in.

"I'm so sorry." "I'm here for you." "Whatever you need."

Where did they all go? They disappeared. Evaporated into thin air. Poof!

No one has called, texted, or emailed. No one has made the effort to check on me. No one has mentioned you. When I'm with people, they pretend like nothing has happened.

But something has happened. You're gone, and you're not coming back. My world is shattered. My heart is broken. I'm in pieces. No one notices. They just step over the rubble and continue on.

I'm not saying that no one has been helpful. Some have.

I'm not saying that everyone is insensitive. Some have been kind and caring.

I'm saying that most people seem to want to wish this away, and the result is that I feel invisible, crushed, and abandoned.

I would love to be able to wish this all away. Is it too much to ask that people just respect my grief?

Losing you was more than enough. I hadn't counted on the betrayal of others.

When we lose a child, it affects more than we may have realized at first. A key strand of our web has been severed and now all of life is unsettled. This loss affects everything. Other strands get strained and stretched. Some might fray under the strain.

Relationships are dynamic. They never stay still. We're always growing closer or more distant, usually in small, hardly perceptible ways. When we lose a child, all our relationships are jostled. Our web will never be the same. We head into a season of grief and pain.

Our relationships become more precious to us and we need the support and love of others during this time. Unfortunately, few people know how to care for a grieving heart. When we don't know what to do, we often end up doing nothing.

The initial loss often results in other losses. People don't come through for us, and we feel hurt, betrayed, or even abandoned. Our sense of loneliness grows, and so does our anger. Our hearts, longing to be seen, heard, and cared for, are further devastated and want to slink away into hiding.

This loss is painful, and grief is a lonely, rocky road. Finding good traveling companions can be difficult and challenging.

No one knows how we feel - even those who have also lost children. It's *our* loss. It is *our* grief – uniquely ours. Others can empathize, but they are not in our hearts and minds. This was *our* child.

When those we counted on don't even bother to show up, angry disappointment is the natural result. We must give ourselves permission to hurt over these new losses. We can find healthy ways to express the anger that comes.

Thankfully, not everyone will disappear. Others we haven't counted on will step forward. New people will surface. We might feel alone, but this grief road is well populated with fellow travelers. Some of them have lost children too. We aren't the only passengers on this roller-coaster.

We breathe deeply. We guard our hearts. We accept that our relationships will change because we are changing. Everything is different.

Affirmation: Though some people might disappoint me,
I will grieve as best I can, given the circumstances.

LOSING YOU IS IMPACTING MY MARRIAGE

FROM THE GRIEVING HEART:

Losing you is impacting all my relationships, especially my marriage.

We're both your parents, but we're dealing with this so differently. I had assumed that this would bring us closer together and that we would cling to each other through this unthinkable tragedy.

But that's not happening. Rather than grieving together, I can feel us drifting apart.

Neither one of us knows what to do. We're both missing you so badly. When one wants to talk, the other doesn't. One of us wants to try this or that to help ourselves heal, while the other doesn't.

You died and then a creeping separateness started to invade our family. No one knows what to do. And what's worse, sometimes we take it out on each other.

It's confusing and frustrating. At the very times we need each other the most, we can't seem to connect. I don't know what to do. I'm hurting and frightened.

It's like your death set off a chain reaction of destruction in our lives.

It can't go on like this. We've got to find a way to come together. We should be walking together in this, grieving together, sharing together, crying together.

Together. That word has more meaning now.

When a child dies, our family changes forever. This change hits our marriage too.

We're different. That's part of what attracted us to each other. We think, feel, and process things differently. We're both one-of-a-kind, unique individuals. We each had a unique relationship with the child we lost.

We both lost a son or daughter. That impacts us differently. Our marriage will never be the same.

No relationship we have will stay the same. This loss changes everything, including us. If we're changing, then of course all our relationships must naturally change as well. We will either grow closer or more distant. We will come closer together, or more separateness will invade.

Our life web has taken a terrible hit. A main strand has been severed. The web is losing its former shape. This can be unnerving and frightening.

Amid all the upheaval, we look for ways to come together with our spouse. We must find ways to be together in this - to grieve together. We both need space, but we both need each other - more than ever before.

Accepting each other is key in this process. We love another person by entering their world and existing with them there. We can do that for our partner, even if they can't seem to do it for us. We can love them by taking care of ourselves - being kind to ourselves and patient with ourselves. We can support them by expressing our grief in healthy ways.

Grief is a moving target. What we need changes day by day and moment by moment. As much as possible, we focus on meeting our spouse where they are, as they are, and being with them there.

Now is not forever. As we express our grief and process it in healthy ways, we will begin to heal over time. We will never be the same, but we can do more than exist and survive. Our grief will change over time, and so will our relationship with our partner.

Our world has changed. We've changed. Our marriage must change too.

Affirmation: Your loss changed everything, including my marriage. Amid the pain, I will focus on loving myself and my partner well. I'll be patient and trust that we will heal and grow through this together somehow.

HOW DO I PARENT MY OTHER KIDS THROUGH THIS?

FROM THE GRIEVING HEART:

My other kids are grieving too. Of course.
Your siblings miss you desperately.

How do I parent them through this?

Sometimes I feel like I must put my grief on hold
in order to be there for them. Their sibling is gone,
and they don't know what to do with that.

I don't know what to do with this either. Life was
already demanding. Now, it's overwhelming.

How do I talk to them about you? What
should I say or not say, do or not do?

I wonder how they're processing this. What are they thinking and
feeling? I can see the grief in their eyes, but I'm clueless about
how to help them with this. I can't even seem to help myself.

I'm terrified of messing this up. Their hearts are so tender.
Mine is too. One moment you were here, and the next
you're gone. How are we supposed to deal with that?

I don't have the time or energy to learn anything new or
develop new super-parenting skills. I'm barely functioning
as it is. Some days just getting out of bed is a major
accomplishment. I feel like a robot going through the motions.

Life is so heavy now. The combo of grief and responsibility are crushing.

I wish you were here. We all miss you.

Parenting is one of life's greatest privileges. It's also one of the most difficult jobs on the planet. When a child departs, it's as if life stops. An emotional grenade went off in our household. Everyone is stunned and debris is everywhere. Family life as we knew it is gone.

Our kids are high on our priority list. We tend to put them above ourselves in many ways. With the loss of a child, our hearts are naturally divided. We're devastated, stunned, and even paralyzed. Yet our other kids call to us. They're crushed too, whether they can express that or not. We feel the tension between our own grief and our other children's needs.

No parent wants their kids to hurt, but the reality is that they will. Disappointments, unwanted surprises, and losses will come. They will experience rejection, failure, and grief. Our job is not to protect them from these things (we can't), but to walk with them through the difficulty and hardship they encounter.

The loss of a sibling is complicated, confusing, and painful. Our job is not to make the grief easier somehow, but instead to model for our kids what it means to grieve in healthy ways. As we're real, honest, and authentic about our own grief, they get the message that it's okay for them to hurt too. Rather than protecting them from our grief, we can find ways to grieve together as a family.

It's not a good idea to try to do all this alone. There is good, helpful support out there to assist us in walking through this time. Local hospices and churches often have grief support available for adults, children, and even the whole family.

We must take our own hearts seriously in all this. If we get the support we need to grieve well and in healthy ways, this will trickle down naturally to our kids. If a plane loses cabin pressure, parents are admonished to put their own oxygen mask on first and then assist their kids. The same is true in grief.

If we get more of what we need in this process, we'll be better able to see what would be helpful to our kids. As we focus on grieving in healthy ways, everyone benefits.

Affirmation: As I take care of my own heart in this grief process, my kids will automatically benefit. As I get what I need, I'll see more clearly what might be helpful to them.

ALL I CAN SEE IS YOU

FROM THE GRIEVING HEART:

I see you in every face. In fact, all I can see is you.

It doesn't matter where I go or what I'm doing. It doesn't matter who I'm with or what's happening.

I see you everywhere.

I see you at home. I see you in the car. I see you on the street, in the grocery store, and in restaurants. You're everywhere.

And nowhere.

I'm not hallucinating. I'm not actually "seeing" you. It's like you've become the lens through which I see the world, and so you're in every single picture. I know you're not here, but I can't seem to think about anything else but you.

This might sound weird, but your absence is the presence that follows me everywhere. Everywhere I go and wherever I am, you're not there.

And you will never be there again. This is too much for a parent's shattered heart to deal with.

I know I'm not going crazy - at least I don't think so. I'm missing you. My heart is expressing itself.

I assumed that as long as I'm here that you would be here too. My heart is clearly far from adjusting to you not being in the world I'm living in.

We were meant to be together. I'm your parent.
You're my child. I will always be your parent.

No wonder I see you everywhere.

Our worlds have been altered forever. The change is traumatic and terribly painful. Our hearts and minds can't handle the onslaught of all this change all at once. We take it in increments. One day, one little bit at a time.

We still hear their voice. We seem to see them everywhere. We're constantly aware of their absence. Our minds naturally put our children where they should be, and when they're not there, our hearts are broken all over again.

It is indeed like our child has become the lens through which we see everything else.

This is natural and common in grief. We long for them. We look for them. We sense both their presence and their absence.

We wake each day to the grief roller coaster. Whatever we have planned, chances are things will not work out exactly that way. Emotions will rise and fall. Memories will come and go. Thoughts will invade, swirl around, and depart again. It feels as if everything is in flux and we're not certain where anything is heading.

We had solid ground underneath us before. Now it feels more like quicksand or thick mud. Our footing is less stable. Things seem to take more time and energy than before. Rather than walking, we're limping - or perhaps even dragging - ourselves along.

Every day is a trek through uncharted territory. It's confusing, because the world looks much like it did and yet nothing feels the same. We have no map for this new place we're in. Nothing could have prepared us for this.

With no map, the only way to travel is one step at a time. Sometimes our minds and hearts are so foggy with grief that one step is all we can see. Everything else ahead is a hazy darkness.

We take one step, and then we can see the next step. As we have courage and energy, we take that next step, and then we can see the next one. It's a slow, arduous process.

Affirmation: Sometimes, I'm barely functioning. I'll be patient with myself. I'll focus on living one moment at a time, taking one step at a time.

FOR REFLECTION AND/OR JOURNALING

MY GRIEVING HEART:

"When I'm alone, I find myself thinking about…"

WHERE ARE YOU?

FROM THE GRIEVING HEART:

Where are you? What are you doing? What do you look like now?

I have lots of questions. I think about you and wonder about everything.

Are you thinking about me? Can you see me? Are you still here somehow but I just can't see you?

Yes, I have many questions. I wish I had some answers.

I know what I would like to believe. I wish I could be sure. I need some certainty right now - something besides you're not here and you're not coming back.

I need to know you're okay. I guess that means I believe you're somewhere, somehow. After all, you're too priceless and special to be gone - completely gone and non-existent, right?

I watched you your whole life. You've always been here, somewhere on the planet. When I woke up in the morning, I didn't even have to think about it. You were here.

Now that you're not here, I think about you all the time. You're the obsession of my mind and heart. I can't let you go. I don't want to.

When I die, will I go to you? Will you meet me there, wherever it is? In the meantime, how do I get through today? I need some certainty here - something I can count on.

What do I know for sure?

You're my child. I'm your parent. You're a gift. I miss you. I love you.

These things I know for sure. These things I will remember today.

The death of a child can throw our entire existence into a tailspin. Questions begin to populate our minds.

Chances are, we have many questions, but very few answers. And the few answers we have are not emotionally satisfying. This is common in times of heavy loss.

When our child was young, we were aware of where they were and what they were doing. They were naturally always on our radar. It was our responsibility to "know."

Now, it feels like we know nothing. Our radars are now silent. Our child is now beyond us knowing exactly where they are and what's happening with them. We naturally wonder about a lot of things.

This is a time of uncertainty. Or so it seems. Everything has changed. The world is different. We're different. Our relationships are different. Our lives can feel unstable. This can be frightening, anxiety-producing, and depressing.

And yet, all this is natural and common for those who have lost children. What felt like a manageable and predictable road is now a huge, dark sinkhole. There is no way around it. We must go through it. We've never been here before or seen anything like this.

Overnight, we went from knowing a lot to knowing nothing. We can feel empty, helpless, and even hopeless.

The reality is that we're already in that sinkhole. It opened underneath us the moment our child died. The only way out of this sinkhole is through it. The terrain is rough, uneven, unpredictable. It's dark in here. There never seems to be enough light to see very far or clearly. Like rock climbing, we move carefully and always keep three points of contact. This journey takes incredible focus and energy.

While moving slowly, one step at a time, we remind ourselves of what we know. We're here. We love them. We're still their parent and always will be. They'll always be our child.

Affirmation: I'm shaken. My world has been upended. But I know this – I am still your parent, and you are still my child. I love you.

WHAT ELSE MIGHT HAPPEN?

FROM THE GRIEVING HEART:

I found myself looking for you again today. It's automatic. It's like you're a part of me and I can't survive without you.

I miss you. Desperately.

I keep coming back to the same question: "How could this happen?"

Then I find myself wondering what else might happen - and to whom.

Frankly, it's terrifying. Anything could happen to anyone at any time. One minute you're here, and the next you're gone. What kind of world is this? Who's next?

I'm scared. Terrified.

I want to take all of us — everyone I care about — and go somewhere safe where nothing bad can happen. No more loss. No more deaths. No more departures. No more pain and grief.

I know there is good all around me, but I can't seem to see it right now. My mind keeps drifting back to you. Like a rubber band, I can distance myself from grief for a little while, only to be snapped back to this unpleasant reality of never seeing you again in this life.

I can't even fathom what I just said. I keep expecting to see you and hear your voice.

How can this be?

Life is not at all what I thought it was.

I miss you. I miss me. I miss us. I miss our family. I miss everything.

We know we'll all die someday. We know all those we love will one day say goodbye and depart. Yet, we shudder to think of such things for very long. We hunker down, hoping to somehow keep death and loss at bay.

Parents expect to die before their children. Even if we don't ever think about this, it's a natural assumption that we operate on from day to day. When a child dies, the shock of the unnaturalness of it all can be ongoing. It's unfair, unjust, and wrong.

If this can happen, what else might?

Our stunned hearts begin to wonder where the next blow will fall. Who? When? Where? How? Fear invades.

Being wired for relationships, it's not surprising we try to avoid loss at all costs. We walk through life unconsciously trying to control people and circumstances to minimize any unpleasantness, hardship, and emotional pain. When loss strikes, and we realize how little control we have, our souls begin to shudder with the possibilities of what might happen next.

With the loss of a child, fear will likely come knocking. A parent's heart can even be terrorized by future what ifs. We can't stop the fear from coming, but if we can recognize and acknowledge it, perhaps we can keep it from taking over and ruling our hearts.

Instead of reacting by trying to run, hide, or deny its presence, we can acknowledge the fear. "I'm afraid." We identify it, if we can. "I'm afraid I'm going to lose another child or someone I love." Simply acknowledging and identifying the fear will help unplug its power.

Losing a child can be terrifying in many ways. Fear will come. It is a natural and common part of grief.

Affirmation: When fear comes, I'll try to acknowledge it, identify it, and release it.

I'M ON EDGE

FROM THE GRIEVING HEART:

I woke up afraid and panicky this morning.

I'm on edge. I'm nervous and on high alert. I'm waiting for the next brick to fall out of the sky on me or another member of my family. I've noticed that my hands tremble sometimes.

I worry more. In fact, I worry about almost everything. I'm checking on people more. I seem to be anxious most of the time.

I had an anxiety attack yesterday. I was walking along minding my own business when fear and panic descended out of nowhere. I got light-headed. My heart began to race. I couldn't get enough air. I felt like I was going to pass out.

I found a place to sit until it passed. It was terrifying. Now I know why they call them panic attacks.

It's as if the grief grows inside me and then breaks out, flooding me with anxiety and fear.

What is happening to me? Am I going crazy? Is this all about you and the huge hole in my heart that I can't seem to fill?

I hate this.

When we feel out of control, most of us experience anxiety. When loss invades, our capacity for handling additional stress becomes more limited. Our world has changed. Our child is gone. Our hearts are struggling to deal with all the unwanted changes that have been suddenly thrust upon us.

We're more nervous than usual. We become hypersensitive to certain things. Our baseline anxiety level rises. Over time, this anxiety can build until our systems are maxed out and can't store anymore. At some point, the dam cracks, and the pent-up emotion begins to spill out.

Anxiety is common in grief, especially after the loss of a child. Many have episodes of intense anxiety or panic. For those who have never experienced an anxiety attack, this can be terrifying. Panic attacks can be horrific.

Breathing becomes crucial at these times. This naturally calms the system, slowing down the mind and lowering anxiety. If we're willing to practice breathing deeply – slowly in through the nose and out through the mouth – at least once a day, we'll be far more likely to do so when anxiety or panic strikes.

Anxiety can derail our sense of well-being. Learning to breathe deeply can be a formidable skill to help us ride the grief roller-coaster better.

We can breathe and be patient with ourselves. This wasn't supposed to happen. No wonder we're anxious.

Affirmation: When anxiety strikes, I'll breathe deeply and remind myself that it will pass.

COULD I HAVE KEPT THIS FROM HAPPENING?

FROM THE GRIEVING HEART:

Surely, I could have done something that would have made a difference.

I lay awake last night, thinking of all I might have done or said differently. Could I have kept this from happening somehow? Perhaps I can do something to bring you back?

Ridiculous, I know. Yet, my heart seems stuck there. Deep down, I believe that this is my fault. I feel guilty.

After all, someone must be responsible, right? And not knowing who that is, it might as well be me.

Is this another form of sadness? Am I mad at myself? Was I in the wrong place at the wrong time? Is this more of me trying to make sense out of what I can't seem to accept?

Strangely, sometimes the guilt feels good. I seem to need a target for this pain, even if that target is me. Otherwise, it all seems completely random and by chance, and that's simply too terrifying for my soul to contemplate right now.

I would rather feel guilty.

When tragedy happens, at first, we're stunned. The loss of a child is shocking. When we come to our senses, we begin to wonder who's responsible for the current situation. We naturally look for someone to blame. Our anger and angst need a target. And often, the most convenient target is us.

After all, we're their parents. We're supposed to protect them. We didn't – or couldn't. The guilt can be heavy and stifling.

Some of us are quite familiar with guilt. We grew up with it. It has been our frequent, often uncomfortable companion. Guilt moves in and unpacks its bags. It makes a home in our hearts.

Guilt is noisy. It's always speaking, filling our minds with its words and subtle accusations. Guilt's voice becomes so familiar, we begin to confuse it with our own.

Yes, it's our fault. It always is.

Guilt may be a frequent guest, but he is not our friend. His accusations and influence profit nothing. Entertaining him too much naturally leads to depression that is more than temporary. Wherever possible, it's best to recognize him, call him out, and send him packing.

Guilt is common and natural in grief. How we respond to it can make a big difference.

Affirmation: Guilt is not my friend. I must find ways to show him the door.

I SAID SOME THINGS I SHOULDN'T HAVE

FROM THE GRIEVING HEART:

I felt nauseated this morning. I don't have a stomach bug. I'm missing you.

Yes, it's that bad. Intense. Penetrating.

I've done some thinking about guilt. I'm honestly shocked at how prevalent it is. Now that I'm looking for it, I see it everywhere. Its fingerprints are all over me.

I said things I shouldn't have. I didn't say things I should have. I know I hurt you, on more than one occasion. I have plenty of little regrets – and a few big ones.

I could have done so much more for you. I could have expressed my love and care more. Surely, I could have protected you somehow.

I could have. I should have. If only I hadn't. If only I had. I wish. What if.

I missed something. If I had done what I should have, you would still be here. At least, that's what I think sometimes.

The guilt list has no end. How can I make these things right? Is that possible?

I get it. Guilt is not my friend, but he is very real right now.

I feel like a failure as a parent. Maybe I am.

How do I deal with this?

When a child departs, we naturally replay everything. We scrutinize what happened and how. We play it over and over in our minds, even if we weren't present at the time. Mental images and internal pictures haunt us.

We look back and review what was said and not said, done and not done. We turn the spotlight on ourselves. We place ourselves in the interrogation room and pepper ourselves with questions. Wounds from the past naturally surface.

Once this terrible loss strikes, our hearts are left to grapple with regrets, mistakes, and failures. Our minds are tortured by missed opportunities and crushed hopes. Our plans and dreams have been shattered.

We want to take responsibility for what we did and said. We want to clear things up and make things right somehow. Our souls squirm under the pressure of unresolved issues and unfinished relational business. This is natural and common.

Many find it helpful to write a letter to their child, expressing their love and their regrets. Asking forgiveness is important and healthy. Though we get no response, confessions like these are good for the soul. If we don't want to write it out, we can speak it. Some set up an empty chair and imagine their son or daughter there. We can ask their forgiveness and express our love.

Getting the grief out is important. If we don't, it can fester inside and begin to infect our life and relationships.

Forgiving ourselves can be hard. Our hearts want to hang on. For some reason, we feel that letting go of guilt means walking away and leaving our children behind. On the contrary, forgiving ourselves can free us to grieve and express our love more authentically.

Now is the time to begin to forgive ourselves. Our children would want this. Our hearts will thank us.

Affirmation: I will ask forgiveness and also forgive myself, so I can be free to love you and grieve well.

FOR REFLECTION AND/OR JOURNALING

MY GRIEVING HEART:

"When I think about guilt and forgiveness, I find myself wondering about..."

PLEASE FORGIVE ME

FROM THE GRIEVING HEART:

Please forgive me. I'm so sorry.

I can almost see you sitting across from me, smiling. Are you telling me it's okay? Are you telling me I'm forgiven and to let it go?

Forgiving myself is hard. Technically speaking, it should be easy. My heart, however, doesn't seem to want to move on.

Move on? I can't believe I just said that. I don't want to move on if that means leaving you behind. That's impossible. You're my child. I'm your parent. You're a part of me.

They say that those who leave are never far from us. I know you're in my heart, and that's close indeed.

Is my reluctance to forgive myself an attempt to hang on to you?

Perhaps I have this backward. If I cling to guilt, I'm making it about me. I want this to be about you and about us. Maybe I need to look in the mirror and into my own eyes and say, "I forgive you."

I know you forgive me. You would want me to forgive myself.

This is hard. Everything seems to remind me that you are gone.

Forgiving ourselves for actual and perceived wrongs is tough duty. Our hearts want to hang on, perhaps in an attempt to keep our child with us. Forgiving ourselves feels like letting go, and that's the last thing we want to do. We don't want to move forward. We would rather back up and have life the way it used to be.

We know what was. We don't know what will be. And right now, we're stuck in the middle, in some weird state of limbo. This emotional roller-coaster is terribly taxing. Getting rid of unnecessary and unwanted baggage can be extremely helpful.

Lack of forgiveness distracts us from loving. Refusal to forgive ourselves hinders healthy grieving. Holding our own hearts captive will not bring our child back.

Perhaps looking in the mirror is a good idea. Saying, "I forgive you," to ourselves can be powerful. Some write down what they feel guilty about and then tear it up and toss it in the trash can or burn it in their fireplace. Others find an object to represent their regrets, grip it tightly, and then intentionally release it.

The key is getting the guilt out. This is part of grieving. Forgiving ourselves is an important life skill.

Affirmation: I will say to myself, "I forgive you."
This is part of loving and honoring you.

IS SOMEONE RESPONSIBLE FOR THIS SOMEHOW?

FROM THE GRIEVING HEART:

Today, I'm feeling angry. Surely someone could have done something. I mean, this didn't have to happen, did it?

I wonder. Is someone responsible somehow, someone beyond me?

If I'm looking for who's potentially at fault, I don't have to look far. Yes, there are people I could be mad at. It would be easy to find a target for my anger.

Why did you have to leave? Did you have any idea of the devastation your departure would cause? You probably have no idea how important you are to me – to all of us.

I'm frustrated. I want to take this out on someone and something, but who and what? In the end, I circle back around to the fact that you're gone, and nothing is going to bring you back.

I admit that the anger feels good. It feels powerful. Perhaps it causes me to feel like I'm doing something, maybe protecting you somehow.

I don't know. Maybe it's enough to say, "I miss you. I'm angry that you left. I'm angry that you're not here. I'm angry you've been taken away."

Our child should be here. They're not. Anger is a natural response.

At some point, most grieving hearts look for someone or something to blame for what happened, even if the death was due to an accident, illness, or disease. Powerful emotions seem easier to express if we have a clearly defined target.

If we're looking to lay blame, finding someone to pin the loss on is easy. There are usually multiple possibilities and no shortage of candidates. Even our children themselves could wind up on the list.

Frankly, we're good at the blame game. Over the centuries we've developed it into an art form. Of course, there are times when specific people are responsible and at fault. In any case, forgiving those we perceive to be in the wrong will be key to our grief process and recovery.

Forgiveness is not saying that it doesn't hurt or that it didn't matter. Forgiveness is saying that it does hurt, it did matter, and we refuse to let what someone else did control our minds, hearts, and decision-making. We often see forgiveness as releasing the guilty party, when instead we're releasing ourselves from an invisible snare.

Our hearts can't afford to keep score. If we do, no one wins. We grow cold inside, and finally bitter. The internal rage shows itself over time, usually in self-destructive ways.

Failure to forgive hurts us, and, by extension, all those connected to us. Bitterness strangles our ability to love.

In other words, we can't afford to not forgive. Our hearts, relationships, and quality of life depend on it. Our children wouldn't want us torturing ourselves with this internal darkness. They would want us free to live and love well.

Affirmation: Blaming won't bring you back. Instead, I'll forgive. I want my heart to be set free from unforgiveness and anger.

I FEEL LOST

FROM THE GRIEVING HEART:

I feel lost.

I don't know what to do. I feel paralyzed. I want to take action, thinking it will help, but I'm terrified of making a mistake or doing the wrong thing.

My confidence seems to have departed with you. My sense of competence is rattled. My security is shaken. I don't feel safe. I wake up in the middle of the night terrified.

I walk around on hyper-alert. I'm waiting for the next hit. Another loss of some kind smacks me every day. I'm losing everything connected to you – past, present, and future. My life is a huge void.

Losing you is like a snowball rolling downhill. The devastation is spreading everywhere and all over everything.

Did you have any idea how huge you were? How much space you occupied? How much influence you had?

You've always been here but now you're gone. How can this be?

I guess it's true. I took so much for granted. We don't know what we've got until it's gone.

I miss talking. I miss your voice. I miss your presence.

I miss everything.

The parent-child bond is deeper than we realize. We become much like two pieces of paper firmly glued together. To attempt to separate them would be disaster. It's virtually impossible. Certainly, neither piece of paper would be the same. Both would be terribly torn.

That aptly describes our hearts. We're deeply attached to our child, even if our relationship had ups and downs. One piece of paper has been torn away, leaving us with gaping holes inside.

Like two pieces glued together, we carry parts of our child with us. Pieces of them are everywhere in our hearts and lives. They live on, in and through us. Their influence is powerful and profound. They shaped our hearts and lives deeply.

We carry them with us even while their absence permeates everything. Their physical presence is gone, and yet they are here - everywhere. This is why we grieve. We miss them and long for them. And yet we sense them and look for them everywhere.

We are all unique, one-of-a-kind individuals. The same is true of our children. There has never been another parent-child relationship exactly like ours, and there never will be again. Stunningly special. Profoundly significant. Absolutely priceless.

Our grief is lonely — and special. We will get through this, but we will not be the same.

Affirmation: I feel lost and lonely sometimes.
This is natural. I'll accept myself and take things
one step at a time, one moment at a time.

I JUST EXIST

FROM THE GRIEVING HEART:

I get up. I move. I go where I'm supposed to and do some of what I'm expected to do.

I see people and interact. I have conversations. I even smile now and then.

Inside, I feel empty. Lost. Numb.

I was wondering how I was going to survive this. I'm not sure I am.

I exist. Barely.

Sometimes I think I'm avoiding the grief. At other times grief feels like my entire existence. I guess something can be so intense that I can numb out.

I'm going through the motions. I do stuff, but I'm not really there. It's like my heart vanished. Perhaps it's with you.

I trust that this is a phase of some kind. I've heard from others that my grief will change over time. I hope so.

And then I come back to the terrible fact behind all of this: you're gone. And then I wonder how the pain can possibly get any better. The problem is that you're not here.

And that's a permanent problem. It's not going to change. What do I do with that?

I need to talk. I need to express what's happening inside to someone somehow. I can't keep this bottled up inside. I'll eventually explode.

We were meant to live, not merely exist.
How do I do that without you?

"I'm just existing." Grieving hearts feel and say this a lot - especially grieving parents.

All of life has suddenly changed. Everything has shifted. Some normal and routine things have disappeared. Some unexpected and unwanted things have invaded. Loss has entered and grief seems to be taking up more and more of our internal space.

The emotional intensity of it all can wear us out. Our hearts power down. We live in a fog. We go here and there, but then forget much of what we saw and did. We function, but much like robots. We feel stiff, mechanical, even unfeeling at times.

We move from living to surviving to existing. Our hearts have been shattered and the pieces are strewn everywhere. We're exhausted. We stare blankly at the pieces but can't imagine having the energy to pick them up. We blink, sigh, and then mechanically do the next thing on the agenda.

This feeling of merely existing is common and natural for a grieving parent. We are limited beings and can only handle so much at any given time. A terrible catastrophe has occurred and we're in the Grief ICU. All we can feel is the pain and the emptiness created by this loss.

Expressing what's happening inside us is critical. We must find ways to get the grief churning within us out and into the open. As we express our grief and process it in healthy ways, the pieces of our hearts will begin to find each other. Over time, we will heal, but we will never be the same.

Though healing may be hard to imagine, it is real and possible. As we do what we know to do to take care of ourselves and grieve well, life will slowly become more than mere existence. At some point, we will begin to smile at memories and live with purpose - loving ourselves, honoring our child, and loving those around us.

Affirmation: I will go through periods where I feel like I'm merely existing. My stunned and shattered heart is expressing its grief. I'll breathe deeply and do what I know to do, one moment, one step at a time.

FOR REFLECTION AND/OR JOURNALING

MY GRIEVING HEART:

"Since losing you, I notice I've also lost…"

OUR FAMILY IS FOREVER CHANGED

FROM THE GRIEVING HEART:

I feel like the world is coming apart. Or at least, it seems like our family is. It's as if you were the glue that held us together.

I know we all have our place. The problem is that your place is empty. I don't know what to do with that. None of us do.

We were a family, but now it feels like we're something else. It's like you've been abducted. Disappeared. You're gone. Poof, just like that.

The ripple effects on all our hearts are massive. Your death was less like a ripple and more like a tidal wave. We're all stunned. We don't know who we are or how to be. When we're together, all we can think about is who's missing.

Our family is not the same. We will never be the same again.

Please forgive me. I took all of that for granted. Which means I took you for granted. I guess I assumed things would go on as they always had, forever.

I don't know what's going to happen to us. Who are we now and who will we be? We can't fill your place. The void you left is permanent. None of us know what to do with that.

You were you. You're irreplaceable.

Our family will never be the same.

When a child departs, the impact on the family web is massive. A central thread running through all the others has vanished. The web immediately loses it consistency and shape. Although the remaining threads are the same, the web is nothing like it was before.

The power of a single thread is stunning. A single person, a single life, has profound, deep impact.

Families do life together, no matter how old our kids are. Even if the relationship is not the best, the connections are powerful and run deep. When a child dies, it can feel like the family web is falling apart and that the remaining threads are separating from each other.

Though this might be frustrating, it's not our job to step in and attempt to replace our child. For starters, that's impossible. What we can do is be ourselves in the moment - authentic and real. We discover that we'll be mourning not only our child, but all their influence within the family as well.

Our family has changed. Therefore, all the relationships within the family will change. Things can't remain the same. Based on a variety of factors, the relationships we have with our other children and relatives will either grow closer or more distant.

Of course, no relationship ever stays the same. Relationships by nature are dynamic and evolving. The loss of a child suddenly forces the family into a different mold and what emerges is a web of different character and shape.

As this new web takes shape, we continue to breathe deeply and do what we know to do to process our grief well and in healthy ways. As we take care of our own hearts, the good that comes out of that will naturally influence the rest of the family as well.

When we take good care of ourselves, we're honoring the child we lost and expressing love to those around us.

Affirmation: A key strand of our family web is gone. Our family will change. I'll focus on processing my grief well.

WHAT DO I DO WITH YOUR THINGS?

FROM THE GRIEVING HEART:

I go into your old room. A shock wave hits.

I sit on the bed and caress the bedspread. I look around. Memories come flooding into my soul.

Every object I lay my eyes on takes me somewhere. Like a series of YouTube videos, scenes play in my head, one after the other.

What am I going to do with your things?

Right now, I don't want to do anything with them. I want them all right here, in their place, where you should be.

My mind begins to spin with possibilities: Get rid of them all. Give them away. Keep a few special things as remembrances. Let other family and friends choose something for themselves. And so on…

No, it's too much. Too much for now. Too much for today.

I caress the bedspread again, sigh, and stand up. The room spins a bit.

All of this has been dizzying for me on so many levels.

Do I close the door? Do I leave it open?

I don't know. I just don't know…

We tell ourselves that possessions don't matter. They are merely things. Technically, this is true. When a child dies, however, their things suddenly become an extension of them. They are no longer with us, but many of their possessions might be.

At first, most of us want to hang on to anything and everything that reminds us of our child. Their presence seems to linger in clothes, objects, and pictures. We quickly discover that certain objects trigger particularly powerful memories. Our child's possessions become representations of them.

At some point, we wonder what we should do with all these things. The word "should" is problematic here. It implies that there is a right or wrong approach to this. Each of us is unique. Our child was unique. Our relationship with them was unique. Our grief process and the timing of certain decisions will be unique as well.

Whatever direction we're leaning, it's probably wise not to make decisions about our child's possessions alone. We need other people in this with us. We need safe people that we trust. People that we know love us and can enter our grief with us.

In addition, decision-making is tough when we're in heavy grief. We simply don't have the usual cognitive abilities or wisdom at our disposal. We need to take our time. There is no rush. We need to do what we sense is best for our own hearts.

The same healthy grieving principles apply here as well. We focus on being kind to ourselves and patient with ourselves. We find healthy ways to express and process our grief. We take care of ourselves. We find meaningful and healing ways to remember our child and honor them. If we let these principles guide us, we will know what to do about our child's possessions when the time comes.

For now, we remember. We caress the bedspread. We touch these possessions packed with personal history and emotion. We let the grief come. We express our love for our child.

Affirmation: As I focus on taking care of myself and grieving in healthy ways, I'll know what to do with your possessions when the time is right. Until then, I'll grieve well and express my love for you as best I can.

I HAVE MORE QUESTIONS THAN I THOUGHT

FROM THE GRIEVING HEART:

What about God? How does he fit into all this?

Couldn't he have done something? If he is good, why doesn't he step in and prevent things like this? Why does anyone have to die?

I have more questions than I thought. Losing you has opened a Pandora's Box inside me. I don't seem to have any answers. Only questions.

And the biggest one of all is, "Why?"

Perhaps I'm angry at God. Eventually, the buck must stop somewhere with someone, right? How could he let this happen?

Maybe my idea of God is muddled. I know I'm confused right now. Not much of anything makes sense.

I'm full of angst and looking for a place to unload it. I'm irritable and cranky. My fuse is incredibly short. Everything bugs me.

I feel small. Tiny. Life seems so big and overwhelming.

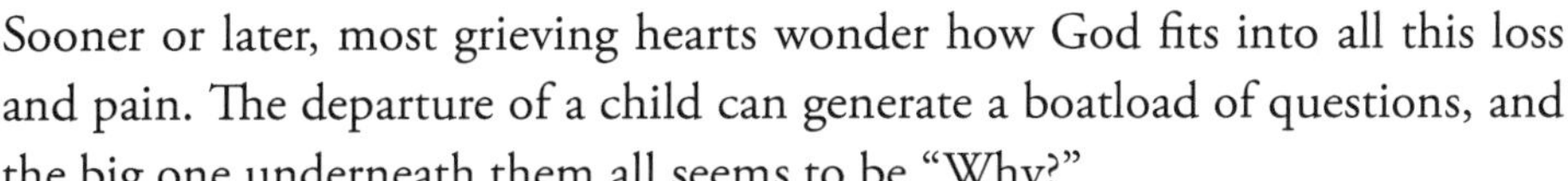

Sooner or later, most grieving hearts wonder how God fits into all this loss and pain. The departure of a child can generate a boatload of questions, and the big one underneath them all seems to be "Why?"

Why them? Why this way? Why now? Why us? Why?

"Why?" is often too big for us. It points to something or someone larger and more powerful than we are. After our minds trace through all the possible reasons why this death and separation occurred, many of us find ourselves pointing an angry finger at God.

Some wonder, "Is it okay to be mad at God?" Whether it's acceptable or not, many people are angry with the one they see as having the power to prevent catastrophe and is therefore, in the end, responsible for it. No matter what our feelings are and towards whom, it's important that we're honest with ourselves about what's happening inside us.

Grief will be expressed, one way or another. The same is true about being angry with God. If possible, it's best to find healthy ways to expel our angst and frustration. We can tell God about it. Speak our feelings. Write them down. Draw them.

If we have a relationship with God, it might be good to remember that the quality of any relationship is based on trust and authenticity. If he is God, he already knows what we're feeling. Be real with him. Share. Let it out. Ask the questions.

Our hearts need to express what's happening inside us. Our grief is expressing our love.

Affirmation: When I'm angry with God, I'll be honest about it. He can handle my emotions.

YOUR LIFE KEEPS FLASHING BEFORE MY EYES

FROM THE GRIEVING HEART:

Every day is a trip through the past. Almost everything reminds me of you. Your life keep flashing before my eyes.

I'm holding you just after you were born. I'm carrying you here and there. I'm playing with you on the floor. Times were simple then.

I see you growing up. Snippets in my mind of you and your friends. Games. Activities. School. Time kept passing and you kept growing.

The pictures and memories keep coming, all the way up to your death. And then my internal video of your life starts all over again.

It's like I'm reliving our life together in bits and pieces. Each scene comes with its own unique variety of reactions and emotions. I smile and then cry. I weep and then laugh. I sigh a lot.

I just want you here. I want you back.

On the one hand, this mental video loop is driving me crazy with sadness and longing. I think I want it to stop, but then I don't. My heart longs to see you, and at least your life playing over and over on my mental screen gives me that opportunity, in a small way.

You're gone, but you're still here. I'm living that contradiction every moment.

Our hearts are memory-central. What comes in through our eyes, ears, and other senses gets stored away, cataloged, and prioritized in its appropriate box. That box gets moved to our memory warehouse. This is going on all the time, even now, at this moment.

For whatever reason, some memories are more powerful and influential than others. These hover at the tops of whatever boxes our brain has filed them away in. Some of these memory boxes are larger than others.

In our memory warehouse there is a special box labeled with our child's name. All our memories of them are there. When a child dies, we automatically run for their box. We throw off the lid, and the memories come spilling out.

It's as if the rest of life stops and all that exists is our child's box. We dig through it. We shuffle the memories here and there. Certain powerful and meaningful ones stand out. We come back to these again and again.

The world knocks and demands our attention. We sigh. We might exit the memory warehouse for a while to do what must be done, but our minds and hearts long to return to our child's box and continue this necessary but painful trip down memory lane.

It's as if our child's life is passing before our eyes - over and over again.

The memories come with all sorts of thoughts and emotions. Sadness. Longing. Anger. Guilt. Frustration. Delight. Confusion. The list goes on and on.

Our hearts are trying to process this unthinkable loss. We go over it again and again. We immerse ourselves in what was. We cling to our internal videos of our child's past, because now that's all we have. Our memories are great gifts. We cling to and cherish them.

Our minds and hearts never stop working. We see our child even in our sleep. We loved them. We love them still.

Affirmation: I'll cherish my memories of you. I will let them come, with whatever emotions they might bring. I'll use these times to remember and be thankful.

YOU WON'T BE HERE

FROM THE GRIEVING HEART:

I find myself thinking about the future. I should say - the future that I was anticipating and now will never be.

I look ahead and see all the things and events you won't be here for. All the things you will miss. All that we will miss because you're not here.

You won't be here as I get older. I won't get to see you get older. Strange. Now you will be forever the age you were when you died. It's as if time stopped somehow.

My mind goes over it again. You won't be here for this. You won't be here for that. No more birthdays, holidays, Thanksgivings, Christmases, or family gatherings. Of course, those days will all come, but the important thing is that you won't be here.

Your siblings will continue to grow, get older, and live life. Your aunts and uncles will keep trudging through their days and living their lives. Your friends will keep living, working, doing life, and getting older. But you - you are frozen in time, my child. You are forever you - then, when death took you.

I don't know how we're going to do this without you. Your absence covers everything. The silence you've left behind is deafening.

I know this you-won't -be-there mode is necessary and a part of my grief. I look forward to the day, however, when I'm less plagued by your future absence and more able to include you in all this somehow - even though you're not here.

I miss you. Desperately.

In the grief process, it's natural and common for us to look ahead and be stunned by what will no longer be. The life we had assumed and anticipated is gone. Our child's departure has shredded our picture of the future.

We can become hyperaware and even obsessed by the important occasions and events our child won't be here for. Birthdays, anniversaries, holidays, and family gatherings. Weddings, graduations, achievements, and milestones. Everyone in our family learning, growing, getting older, and doing life together. Our child will be absent from all of this.

We grieve over what they will miss. We're stunned and shattered by what we will miss because they're not here. It's like someone threw a grenade into our family. We're stunned by all the alterations, debris, and destruction that seems to surround us. One departure has massive impact. The ripple effects go on and on.

When at a planned gathering or event and we suddenly notice we haven't seen someone we expected to be there, we naturally wonder, "Where are they?" In our minds, they should be there. Now, "Where are they?" is a constant question, a new but permanent resident in our hearts.

Yes, this you-won't-be-there phase is necessary and healthy. Our worlds have changed. The future has changed. We have changed. Everything is different now. What once was perhaps a predictable picture of the future is now in tatters and unrecognizable. That picture no longer exists, but our hearts are not ready to construct another one yet.

So, we look ahead and grieve. We grieve what will be missed - by both our child and us. We mourn in advance the events and places where they will not be. In the present, we're missing their presence in the future.

We didn't want this change. We didn't ask for it. It invaded. Now we've been thrust into a new, unfamiliar world. It's like we must learn how to do life, all over again.

Affirmation: I'm missing the life I planned that will no longer be. I'm missing you both now and in the future. I miss you because I love you. I will be patient with myself through this.

FOR REFLECTION AND/OR JOURNALING

MY GRIEVING HEART:

"If I were to catalog what's been helpful and what hasn't in my grief process, I would say…"

THE VOID THAT YOU'VE LEFT IS MASSIVE

FROM THE GRIEVING HEART:

Since you left, I'm not the same. I used to love going places and being with people. I loved fun as much as the next person.

All that has changed. For me, all the fun seems to have been sucked out of the universe. Life feels heavy. Walking through my day is like slogging through waist-deep mud.

You're gone. How can I have fun?

I don't want to go anywhere. I don't want to see anyone. I want to be alone. I'm hurting, and I would prefer to hide.

Everywhere I go, I feel people looking at me. I assume they're wondering how I'm doing, or maybe what to say or do. It seems like I make everyone uncomfortable.

My heart can't handle it. If I'm alone, I don't have to worry about others, what they're thinking, what I need to do, how I'm coming across, etc. I'm not prepared for judgment or criticism, and I'm afraid that's exactly what I'm going to get.

I've had enough blank stares and judgmental looks. People just don't get it.

I'll revel in my sadness and miss you all I want. Your absence covers my world. The void you have left is massive.

I miss you.

The loss of a child stuns us. The emotional onslaught of sadness, anger, anxiety, confusion, guilt, and frustration can be intense. Life becomes heavy. Fun disappears. Laughter seems out of place, unloving, or even irreverent.

The world looks different. Some of us become overly aware of what others might be thinking about us and our grief. Being in public or with others socially can become difficult. We're not on the same page as everyone else, and we feel that keenly.

For many, the safest and most logical thing to do is to go home and stay there.

When we're wounded, we naturally tend to withdraw. Instinctively, we know we need to heal. Recovery from a deep, traumatic loss like this requires time for us to think, feel, battle internally, and adjust. And some of this is best done alone.

Yes, we need other people, but most of us also need quality time alone when grieving. This balance is unique to everyone and is as individual as every loss and each person's grief process. Time alone can be refreshing and healing. Short times of solitude remove the clamor and noise of a world that might be less than helpful to us right now.

The challenge is finding the balance of getting healthy time alone while staying connected to other people. In terms of what we need at any given moment, this balance between solitude and socializing can change in an instant. Grief is an unpredictable moving target.

Our goal is to stay flexible and pay attention to what our hearts might need from moment to moment.

We breathe deeply. We open our eyes and take the next step, however small. One step, one moment at a time.

Affirmation: I'll grieve well by getting the alone time I need while staying connected to people that are helpful to me.

I DON'T FEEL SAFE ANYMORE

FROM THE GRIEVING HEART:

I miss you. I still have trouble believing you're gone. It just doesn't seem real somehow.

I've known you since your first heartbeat, your first breath. How can it be that you're no longer here?

I find I'm more nervous now. My anxiety is up. Honestly, I don't feel safe anymore.

Strange. I never thought of you as part of my sense of safety. Or perhaps my stability has been upended by the fact that this happened – that it even could happen.

I'll always be your parent. I can't stop just because you're gone. And you'll always be my child, no matter where you are.

What kind of world do I live in where this can happen? I know that children die every day, all the time. It's unfathomable. I can't seem to take it in. Perhaps I don't want to.

Losing you is not just sad. It's also frightening, confusing, and unnerving.

My world is not the same. Someone has removed it from its axis or tilted it in another direction. The natural order of things has been upended. It's as if life is a completely different game now, and I have no idea what the rules are.

Sometimes all I seem to feel is your absence. You leave and all the world becomes empty.

How important and special you are, my child.

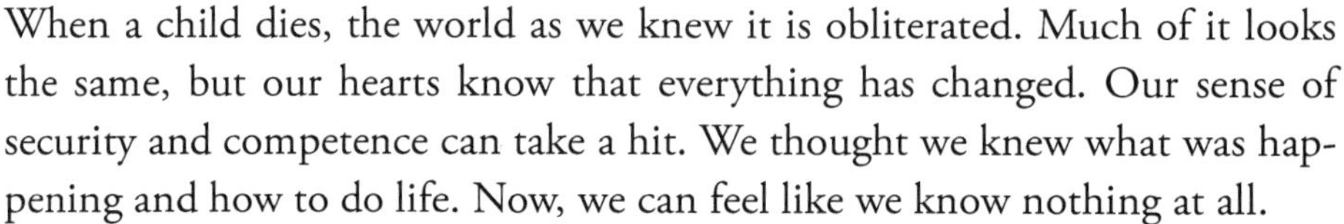

When a child dies, the world as we knew it is obliterated. Much of it looks the same, but our hearts know that everything has changed. Our sense of security and competence can take a hit. We thought we knew what was happening and how to do life. Now, we can feel like we know nothing at all.

We've now experienced the unthinkable. We knew that children die, but not our children. A parent's worst nightmare has become our reality. If this can happen, what else might?

We blink. We wonder what happened and how. We're paralyzed. We move in a daze. We go through the motions.

Stability is gone. Our sense of safety can suddenly evaporate. If our child wasn't safe, then neither are we. No one is truly safe. The world isn't what we thought it was.

Things suddenly feel shaky, uncertain, and unpredictable. Our heart's safety net has been removed.

When something vanishes, we naturally look for it. We know our child is gone, but we search for them in many ways. A basic relationship in our life is now gone. A gaping black hole of emptiness emerges where our safety net used to be.

It doesn't matter how old we are or how old our child was. They are our child and always will be. We are forever their parent.

They are still our child and we are still their parent. This will never change. But we no longer have access to them physically, and that's disturbing and heartbreaking.

We continue to express our love by processing our grief. We talk out loud about them. We share. Perhaps we journal what's happening inside us or write them letters. Maybe we grieve by drawing or painting.

Over time, as we grieve, our sense of safety will most likely return, but it will be different. Everything is different now. This differentness proclaims how important and significant our children are.

Affirmation: It's natural if my sense or safety is rattled for a time. With your departure, nothing seems normal or safe anymore. I'll breathe deeply and keep processing all this as best as I know how.

I FEEL LIKE A SHADOW

FROM THE GRIEVING HEART:

I miss you. Your departure has stolen my appetite. I'm never hungry. I forget to eat. I'm dropping weight.

When I do eat, nothing tastes good. I have no desire to eat anything healthy. Am I punishing myself somehow? Is missing you killing my taste buds?

Eating has become one more thing I don't have energy for. Preparation, cooking, and even chewing are draining. My battery is dying, and I have no idea where the charger is.

I know this isn't good, but I don't care. I don't have energy to care much about anything.

All I seem to be able to care about is missing you.

I sigh a lot. I stare mindlessly into space. I drive places and then have no idea how I got there. Sometimes, I wind up someplace familiar, but not where I intended to go.

I feel like a shadow – a phantom flitting silently through everyone else's world.

I function, sort of. I go through the motions. I get stuff done, but I'm not all there. My heart is with you – thinking about and missing you. When you left, you took a large part of me with you.

Tell me this won't last forever. I know I need to eat, but my heart is starving for you.

Grief is a form of stress. As such, it tends to dull the senses. Our brains think we're under attack and shift our systems into fight-or-flight mode. Our hearts prioritize. When in battle, food is not on the top of our necessity list.

Perhaps meals were times of intimate conversation and connection with our child. If so, every time we eat might be a trip down memory lane.

Grief hits the appetite. It can deaden the taste buds. Most of our energy is focused on emotional survival, and our bodies often pay the price.

We're not hungry, so we forget to eat. We're not thirsty, so we neglect to hydrate. We feel tired, even weak. Over time, our clothing gets looser. We notice changes in the mirror. We begin to lose weight.

Of course, this can go the other direction as well. We can overeat in an effort to comfort ourselves. We sense something lacking inside, so we try to fill that void.

We're usually aware of all this, but we don't have enough emotional energy to care. Apathy comes knocking, and usually gains entrance for a while. We feel like our lives are shrinking, as if we're slowly fading away.

In most cases, this will pass with time. As we process the loss and feel the grief, our appetite will eventually bounce back. We'll begin to taste our food again. Though it may be hard to imagine, our energy and motivation will one day return.

Thankfully, now is not forever.

Affirmation: I'll try to eat well and take care of myself. My child would want this.

I'M EXHAUSTED

FROM THE GRIEVING HEART:

I'm exhausted.

I wake up each day and sigh. My body feels heavy. Everything takes so much effort. Brushing my teeth is a workout.

Not sleeping well doesn't help. Not eating well doesn't help either. My head feels like it's stuffed with cotton. My eyes hurt.

I live in a daze. It's like I'm sleep-walking through life.

Missing you is exhausting. My heart is deflated. Part of me left with you. I don't feel whole.

What's wrong with me? I don't feel like myself at all. Who am I now? I don't recognize this world without you in it. I don't know who I am without you.

I'm so tired I can barely think. I manage to gear up for what I must do, and somehow function enough to get through it. Then I crash on the other side. I zone out for minutes at a time.

I hope this gets better.

Grief demands incredible energy. Life in fight-or-flight mode is exhausting. Fatigue is natural and common during times of loss.

If someone was hit by a bus, we wouldn't expect them to jump up and carry on as usual. If they survived the collision, they would be transported to a hospital, preferably to one with a trauma center, for emergency lifesaving treatment. Once their life is out of danger, the stabilizing process takes time.

Then the healing and recovery process can begin. During this time, all their physical energy is being channeled toward simply staying alive. Fatigue and exhaustion are routine fare for those recovering from life-threatening injuries.

We've been hit by the Grief Bus. Our child is gone. This loss stuns and flattens us. We don't simply shake the collision off and walk away unscathed. Our wounds are invisible but real. The emotional pain is intense and draining. Pain, in any form, taxes our system and exhausts us.

Rest becomes a priority. Fatigue takes a toll over time.

We simply can't do as much. Our performance at work might be off. We need more space and margin in life than ever. Taking ourselves and our grief seriously is critical. Being patient with ourselves is important. Like other grief challenges, the fatigue will change over time.

Our hearts, souls, and bodies will adjust and recover, though we wonder how and when. Time doesn't heal all wounds, but healing does take time.

Affirmation: Grief is exhausting. I'll try to have realistic expectations of myself during this time.

I'M NOT FINE

FROM THE GRIEVING HEART:

Wearing a mask is exhausting. No wonder I don't want to be with people much right now.

I'm sad. Everyone wants me to be happy. I'm irritable, and people close to me wonder why. Others ask how I am. Do they really want to know?

No, I don't think they do. So, I say, "I'm fine."

I'm not fine. And apparently, it's not okay to not be okay. People seem to get upset because I'm grieving. I miss you. Can't they understand that?

I'm learning to hide. It's like I'm on stage playing a role. I thought it might be better to keep the emotions inside when around others but stuffing them away and trying to hide them can be totally exhausting for me. It's like I'm having to separate from myself and my own heart.

I feel like a hypocrite. I don't enjoy being fake, but at the same time, I don't want to be emoting all over everyone and everything either.

I'm caught, stuck, and frustrated. If I must wear a mask, then I must also find safe places where I can take it off.

Missing you is complicated. How do I live on without you here?

We're wired to love and be loved, and that requires honesty and authenticity. Most of us strive to be real, but none of us are completely ourselves with everyone we meet. We're naturally more vulnerable and open with those we trust – the people we know that love and accept us for simply who we are.

In other words, all of us wear masks from time to time, depending on where we are, who we're with, and the state of our own hearts. Some masks, of course, are thicker than others.

The loss of a child and the resulting grief pose a special challenge because the world around us typically doesn't respond well to emotional pain and suffering. We run from grief rather than drawing closer to it. We decide what's most appropriate for any given situation and we act accordingly.

Our grief, however, will not be boxed that conveniently. Though we can hide it momentarily, it refuses to be silenced. The heart will express itself, one way or another.

Grieving well is not about getting rid of all our masks. It's about finding a few people we can be real and honest with — people with whom we can share our pain, frustration, and confusion. We need to feel safe. Our hearts need to be heard.

We're missing our child. Life without them is hard, perhaps even impossible, to imagine.

Affirmation: I will be myself and express my heart with those I trust and feel safe with. I will honor you by sharing my grief.

FOR REFLECTION AND/OR JOURNALING

MY GRIEVING HEART:

"If I were to meet someone who has just lost a child, I would..."

MAYBE I NEED HELP

FROM THE GRIEVING HEART:

Maybe I need help.

I feel stuck. I'm going in circles. My mind spins.

My emotions are volatile and can be overwhelming. They're intense and unpredictable.

My relationships are weird. Everything seems to be changing.

I miss you so badly it physically hurts.

And I'm tired. So very tired.

I try to be strong, but I feel so weak. Perhaps strength isn't what I thought it was. It takes huge amounts of energy to keep all my masks in place. Perhaps dropping them would be easier.

At least, if I can find people I can be real with, that might take the edge off.

I need someone who knows about this stuff and can guide me on this up-and-down, back-and-forth journey of learning to live life without your physical presence. I need someone who will listen and hopefully hear my heart. I need perspective. I need an objective voice from the outside.

Maybe it's time to reach out. But how do I find someone like this?

In times of heavy loss, we all need help. None of us can do this alone and stay healthy and sane. We're made for connection and designed to walk together with others, especially in the tough times. The loss of a child is certainly one of these times.

There comes a point for some of us - perhaps most of us - where supportive friends and family aren't enough. For those of us who don't have particularly supportive people around them, we might be acutely aware of the need for a wise, safe person to give us perspective and reassurance.

Perspective and reassurance. These are two things a grieving parent desperately needs.

Our loss can give us tunnel vision. Everything becomes about our child and about their death. Over time, we need to begin to see this tragedy in the context of the larger picture of life. It usually takes a more objective, outside voice to help us do that. At some point, we need to be able to see things with more balance. We need perspective.

The death of a daughter or son also fills our lives with wondering and seemingly unanswerable questions. Everything gets called into question. Life becomes a thick fog bank and we have trouble even seeing the way forward. We can feel hopeless and helpless. We need to know if what we're enduring is normal or whether we're going crazy. We need reassurance.

Thankfully, there are people out there who can give us these twin gifts. A wise friend or mentor who knows grief well can speak to our hearts with knowledge, compassion, and sensitivity. A counselor or grief professional can be a safe listening ear and an excellent sounding board. Our hearts desperately need the perspective and reassurance that an experienced, wise, and objective person can provide.

Reaching out for such help can be scary - even terrifying. We might feel embarrassed or even ashamed that we can't seem to navigate all this on our own. We've been wounded deeply. Coming out of our shell and trusting someone new (or anyone, for that matter) with our heart can be unnerving.

Most of the best things in life are scary. Good things usually require courage and action. A bereaved parent's heart needs perspective and reassurance. There are people out there who give us that. Perhaps it's time to reach out and find them.

Affirmation: I need perspective and reassurance. I'll find someone who can mentor me through this. Asking for help is a sign of strength, not weakness.

MY OTHER KIDS DON'T UNDERSTAND

FROM THE GRIEVING HEART:

My other kids don't understand. I guess I can't expect them to. They're not your parent.

They keep wanting me to feel better. They keep trying to take care of me. They intervene where I don't want them to. Sometimes I feel nagged, micromanaged, and smothered.

I need to talk about you. They need to talk about you too. How come no one brings you up or shares stories? Why are we avoiding the grief we're all feeling?

I've known you all your life. I'm connected to you in ways that even I don't understand or fathom. Now you're gone, and I miss you desperately. I miss your presence.

Can't my other kids understand that I can't just pick up and move on as if you never existed? They can't either. Are they hiding from their grief?

I try to guess what you might say to them, if you could. It would probably be something like, "Why are you all acting so weird? Talk to each other. Be real."

I want to grieve. I need to grieve. So do they.

This is all so confusing. Your departure changed everything. Our family is different now. There's a massive hole where you used to be.

Perhaps we're all just stressed and none of us knows what to do.

Yes, that's probably it. Breathe. I need to breathe.

Our children love us and mean well. On some level, their hearts have been broken too. We've lost a child. They've lost a sibling. Like us, they don't know what to do with all this. This loss can be complicated and confusing.

We like to feel in control. As a result, we're big on taking action. We want to "do something" to feel better, move along, and somehow get out of the emotional pit that we've been thrust into.

Unfortunately - or fortunately - we're not in control. We don't control what happens next, how, or to whom. We don't control people, situations, or circumstances. About all we have control over are the thoughts we allow to take up residence in our minds and the resulting words and actions.

It's hard for children to watch their parents hurt, and vice versa. Our "fixer" genes get activated, and the temptation is to bustle around and try to make things better somehow. Deep down, however, we know there is no fixing this.

Our other kids are grieving too. It would be nice if we could somehow grieve together. As parents, we can lead in this. As we grieve openly and authentically, we model for our children, no matter how old they are, how to process pain and loss in healthy ways. This is a huge life skill that they will need again, and again.

Loss is hard. The loss of our child strikes the entire family web. Everything is altered. Being patient with ourselves and our other kids becomes one of our new priorities.

We breathe deeply. We take care of ourselves and focus on grieving the loss of our son or daughter in healthy ways. This is the best gift we can give to our other children right now.

Affirmation: I'll recognize that your departure changes all our family relationships. This is stressful and confusing. I'll be patient with myself and all of us in this process.

I KEEP GETTING SURPRISED

FROM THE GRIEVING HEART:

I've heard some things that bother me. Apparently, you didn't tell me everything.

I keep getting surprised, here and there, by things I didn't know. Things you said. Things you did.

I can't help but feel betrayed somehow. Did you lie to me? Or did you just keep things from me? If so, why?

I try to discipline my mind about this, but I can't help wondering what else I don't know. How deep did the hiding go — and to what extent?

I'm angry about this - and deeply disappointed. I thought I knew everything about you. That sounds ridiculous when I say it. No one know anyone else completely.

You are entitled to have your own life, your own thoughts, and your own emotions. I don't need to know everything. I don't want to know everything. Now, I wish I didn't know what I know now.

I need to talk to someone about this. This is eating me up inside. I have to get this out - talk it out, write it out, or something. And I know I have to let this go and forgive you. I'm just not ready to do that yet.

I never expected this to be part of my grief process.

After the loss of a child (especially an adult child), sometimes we hear or discover something about them that we didn't know. Something they said or did. Something they didn't say or didn't do that we were under the impression that they had done or accomplished. Perhaps we discover a secret that disturbs us. This sets off a chain reaction of wondering.

What else might have happened? What else don't we know? What else was hidden that is waiting to be revealed?

Most of all, our trust can be challenged. We naturally assume that we know our children well and that they are exactly who we think they are. This is a natural expectation, even if it's perhaps a bit unrealistic. No one knows another's heart entirely. No one shares absolutely everything.

In addition to this, not every report can be trusted either. We all have selective hearing. What someone heard our child say may not be necessarily what they said or what they meant.

Most kids don't share everything with their parents. There are times when adult children may not share something thinking that they are protecting us. The reality, of course, is that this often backfires. Our hearts respond better to truth, even if it's scary and painful, rather than discovering something later that we wish we had known.

In any case, those of us left behind get to navigate this minefield we didn't know existed. Some general grief principles apply:

Be careful what we listen to. Our hearts are wounded and vulnerable.

Find healthy ways to express what we're thinking and feeling. We must continually "get it out."

Forgive as quickly as possible - whether that means our child, others, or ourselves.

We can also consider whether we have been totally honest with our child along the way. Did we share everything with them? Probably not. If we died and they were the ones left behind, would they discover things about us that might disturb them?

We get surprised in grief, again and again. We breathe deeply. We process what's happening inside. We guard our own hearts. We confide in safe people.

We forgive so that our hearts are not controlled by what cannot be changed.

Affirmation: If I discover something I didn't know that disturbs me, I will guard my heart. I will be honest with myself and try to process that information well.

HOW MUCH MORE AM I GOING TO LOSE?

FROM THE GRIEVING HEART:

Losing you wasn't a one-time thing. It goes on and on.

I can't watch some movies now. There are places I can't go and people that are hard for me to be with. Some foods and aromas set me off. It seems like everywhere I go something reminds me of you.

I didn't only lose you, I lost most of what is connected to you. Anything that surfaces memories of you is painful right now. You touched everything in my life.

It feels like I'm losing everything. I know that's not true, but it sure seems that way. Life as I knew it is slipping through my fingers every moment. I try to grasp what I can and hold it close, only to find myself clinging to empty air.

When will the losses stop? When will the grief end? When will the pain subside?

I'm a walking ball of grief. I can almost feel it oozing out of my pores onto the ground around me. I've lost so much that it's hard to figure out who I am now.

I'm not who I was, I know that much. How much more am I going to lose?

Grief is never simply about one loss. When a son or daughter dies, the ripple effects begin. When this massive, central strand of our life-web is severed, the whole web reverberates with the shock. Some strands are stretched, while others might break. This one loss leads to many other losses.

The loss of a child touches everything. All of life is affected. Some call this collateral damage. The result is that we not only grieve the departure of our son or daughter but of many other things as well.

Certain places, people, events, activities, foods, smells, and music can now pack a grief punch. Anything can be an emotional trigger.

The goal is not to avoid potential triggers, but rather find healthy ways to handle such situations when they arise. Realistically, much of life may remind us of our child, so finding ways to grieve well amid routine daily life is important.

Rather than trying to figure out what's happening – which is difficult during moments of heavy emotion – we can simply try to feel what comes and be honest with our own hearts. We let the grief come, as much as we can, given where we are and who we're around.

Our child touched us in so many ways. They are a basic, foundational, and powerful influence in our lives. Grieving their loss is an on-going, up-and-down process.

Affirmation: I not only lost you but much of what was attached to you. I will try to be kinder to myself because this is hard.

I'M FRUSTRATED WITH PEOPLE

FROM THE GRIEVING HEART:

This is hard.

Losing you was more than enough. All the additional stuff trailing along behind your departure is becoming unbearable.

I'm frustrated with people. They don't get it, and I know they can't. I don't expect them to. But a little common courtesy would be nice. If you don't have something kind and beneficial to say, well, be quiet!

Other people tell me to calm down. "They don't know what to say, but they mean well. Give them a break."

Great. What am I supposed to do? Put up with it, no matter what's said? Confront what's said and express myself? Stay away from such well-meaning but unhelpful people? Maybe stay away from people altogether?

Grieving is hard enough without feeling like I must educate everyone around me about loss and pain. I guess I think certain truths are obvious. We love. People die and leave. A child dying before a parent is weird, complicated, and feels all wrong. We parents are never the same again. What's so hard to understand?

Surely, they have lost a loved one at some point. How can they be so clueless?

Yet, I know that if they haven't lost a child themselves, they have no way of getting to where I am. They have no way of even being able to empathize. Sympathizing is the best they can do.

It's difficult being patient and kind when
you feel whacked and judged.

Breathe. I must breathe.

We're made for connection, but relationships are hard. Good relationships demand attention, nurturing, and work to continue to grow and deepen. People can be difficult and unpredictable, especially when in the presence of emotional pain.

As has been mentioned before, most of what a person says is about them and what's happening inside their hearts. Most of us make almost everything about us. We're in our own skin, acutely aware of how our surroundings – including people and what they say and do – are affecting us at any given moment.

Can grieving hearts expect to be understood by the world around them? No. But it would be nice if the people in our sphere were respectful and considerate. The burden of being misunderstood and invisible, on top of the loss itself, can be crushing.

The truth is that no one else can fully understand what we're going thorough and the pain we're experiencing. Those who have lost children can empathize. They are traveling the same road we are. But this was our child, not theirs. The loneliness of it all can be debilitating. We can find ourselves withdrawing.

Isolating ourselves to avoid more potential pain isn't wise. We need people, connection, and interaction. We might find it helpful to come up with a few canned responses when someone says something insensitive. This allows us to respond in a planned fashion at a time when emotions may muddle our thinking.

Grieving hearts must keep breathing and take themselves seriously.

Affirmation: I can't expect others to understand my grief, but I will work to find some who will be respectful and considerate.

FOR REFLECTION AND/OR JOURNALING

MY GRIEVING HEART:

"Since losing you, I sense my relationships are changing. For example…"

MISSING YOU IS MAKING ME SICK

FROM THE GRIEVING HEART:

I miss you, and I think it's making me sick.

I can't seem to fight off colds like I used to. My stomach hurts. I get headaches from time to time. I'm always tired. My body aches.

Missing you is bad enough but feeling this way on top of it all is frustrating and confusing.

Am I sick? Is there something wrong with me physically? Do I need to go to a doctor?

I don't want to go much of anywhere, least of all to the doctor. I don't want to be poked, prodded, or stuck right now. Life is uncomfortable enough already. I don't want another person, even if it's my doctor, asking me how I'm doing, how I'm coping, or how whatever.

I don't need more questions. I need answers.

My head is full. My mind flits here and there. My heart races from time to time. My shoulders are heavy. I can't seem to get the rest I need. I'm still not eating well.

I'm a mess.

When we lose a child, it affects our entire system. The grief impacts us emotionally, physically, mentally, and spiritually. Many of us experience new or uncomfortable physical symptoms.

Stomach distress, headaches, aches and pains, frequent illnesses, palpitations, racing heartbeat, nausea, and dizziness are common. We can become clumsy, forgetful, and lethargic. Our bodies feel heavy. Daily life takes much more energy.

Grief is stressful. It suppresses the immune system. We get sick more often. Our bodies feel the pain of our loss and express this in a variety of ways. Weird physical symptoms often come with riding the grief rollercoaster. If something concerns us, however, it's important to get it checked out. We don't need the stress and pressure of additional unknowns right now. Grieving hearts often need support, information, and reassurance.

Our bodily distress honors our child. We love them, and we experience their absence in multiple ways.

Rest, proper nutrition, and appropriate exercise are especially important right now.

None of us is perfect — not even close. We simply do the best we can in the situation we find ourselves in.

Affirmation: Grief is hitting my body, too. I'll be kind to myself and take the best care of myself possible.

NO ONE AND NOTHING CAN FIX THIS

FROM THE GRIEVING HEART:

Why do people say the things they do?

I choose to believe that they mean well, but sometimes what's said isn't helpful.

"It's okay." I've heard that a lot. No. Sorry. It's not okay. You're not here anymore, and I'm hurting. How can that be okay?

"Don't worry. You'll get past this." Past what? Past feeling this? Past hurting and grieving?

"At least you had them as long as you did." What does that mean? How long is long enough?

"I know how you feel." How? You're not me. It wasn't your loss or your child. You don't know what's happening inside me.

Ugh. Maybe people think they need to say something. I don't know. It seems like they all want me to feel better. "Stop grieving!" is what my heart ends up hearing.

It's my heart, my life, my loss, and my grief. Why do people try to fix the unfixable?

You're gone. No one and nothing can fix that.

By nature, grief is lonely. We all experience loss, yet each person and relationship are unique. Others who have lost a son or daughter can perhaps empathize, but no one knows the intricacies of another's heart. Grief is a deeply personal and individual process.

Those who haven't lost a child might be terrified of even relating to us. The unthinkable has happened to us. Now they know it could happen to them too. Being around us triggers their fears. Though they try to be polite, many of them try to keep a safe distance from this heartbreaking, soul-shaking loss.

As a result, we often feel alone. Our child was special. Our grief will be special as well.

Well-meaning people often end up saying unhelpful things. We can even feel evaluated, judged, and belittled by others. Grieving hearts are frequently misunderstood.

Though everyone experiences grief, we don't seem to understand it very well. We expect it to be quick – a brief rest stop on life's superhighway. We want grief to be momentary and easily resolved.

Granted, no one wants to hurt or to watch another person suffer. We would wish such emotional hardship away if we could. No wonder we fill the air with words, hoping to make a difference and bring some relief.

Unhelpful and even hurtful things will be said. For our own sake, we need to release such comments quickly and try to keep them from taking up residence in our hearts. Learning to forgive quickly is a healthy skill for grieving souls.

Affirmation: When unhelpful, insensitive words are said, I will protect my heart and release them as quickly as possible.

RELATIONSHIPS ARE MORE COMPLICATED THAN I THOUGHT

FROM THE GRIEVING HEART:

Relationships are turning out to be more complicated than I thought.

I've concluded that most people don't know what to do with grief. Or maybe it's just me and the way I'm grieving.

I was accosted by a couple of advice-givers yesterday. They told me what I should be doing, how, and with whom. Then they wished me well and disappeared. An emotional hit-and-run. I stood there, stunned. Then I went to my car and cried.

To top it all off, neither of these people have experienced a significant loss in their lives, much less the loss of a child.

Why can't people accept where I am and simply be kind? Don't bludgeon me with words. Be with me where I am. See me. Listen to my heart.

I'm hurting. I feel vulnerable. My emotions are all over the place. I could use a few kind people who happen to be great listeners.

I need to talk about you. I miss you terribly.

Our world is full of fixers. These folks are on a mission to evaluate others and correct whatever they determine is wrong or lacking. Fixers often walk away feeling like they've done their part, while the recipient of their suggestions feels criticized, judged, or even attacked.

"You should," "You must," and "You need to..." are key phrases in their repertoire. Most fixers are far more willing to help others tackle their issues rather than deal with their own. In many cases, their attempts to fix our grief is a signal that they're trying to run from theirs.

We're shattered. Devastated. We need people who will simply be with us, where we are, as we are. We need kind and safe people to show up, look us in the eye, and listen. It's their presence that's most valuable, not their words.

It's worth remembering that what others say to us is far more about them than about us. They're unconsciously expressing how they feel about how they perceive we're doing. If possible, limiting our exposure to fixers is important.

Affirmation: Some will try to fix me and my grief. I will remember that their words are usually more about them than about me.

I NEED PEOPLE WHO KNOW GRIEF

FROM THE GRIEVING HEART:

I need people who know grief.

Most of those I see and interact with don't get it. They can't. They haven't lost a child. Many of them haven't even had a significant loss.

I need someone who gets it. Someone who understands. I don't expect them to know how I feel. That's impossible. Plus, my feelings are unique because our relationship was unique. But I need someone who's been through something similar who can empathize and relate.

Where do I find these people? I know they're out there. They have to be.

Perhaps I could look online. What do I search for? Parents who have lost children? Support groups for grieving parents?

The last thing I want to do is go to a group - a bunch of new people I don't know when I'm feeling this vulnerable. I'm not convinced it would help. Then again, I don't know. Such groups exist for a reason, right? Someone must be getting something good out of them.

When I think of interacting with someone who gets it, well, it's almost too good to be true. Like a nice dream of some kind. Weird. Am I trying to isolate myself?

I guess it's natural that after losing you I would try to protect myself any way possible. My heart is broken and the rest of me is tottering on the edge of some unknown cliff.

I need a safety net. I think that's going to be other people - people who understand.

We're relational creatures. That's why this loss hurts so much. We were connected to our child, and now our sense of that connection has been disrupted and severed. The pain is excruciating.

We're designed to do life with others. In this time of heavy grief, we need other people in our lives who know something about child loss. We need other parents who have experienced what we're going through. We need people who we can look in the eye and know that they get it.

These are people who can give us some much-needed perspective and reassurance. They are traveling the same road and facing many of the same obstacles. We need people who will let us mention our child's name and talk about them. Other bereaved parents are great candidates.

Grieving parents can find each other by "accident." It might be a current coworker or acquaintance that we didn't know had experienced this terrible loss. They hear our story and come close. They make themselves known. Suddenly we have an instant and deep bond.

Bereaved parents often find each other in support groups. Some are fans of such groups, while others aren't. Ironically, most of the critics of support groups have never actually been to one. Most of those who have been to such groups, however, testify clearly to how helpful, comforting, and healing being with others going through something similar can be.

When we're hurting like this, any form of reaching out seems threatening and scary. We're already exhausted and drained. We're on "energy save" mode all the time. Checking out a support group seems like one more thing that's going to require energy we don't have.

And yet, those who breathe deeply, set their minds to reach out, and make the first step usually reap great benefits. Just making the call can be huge. Showing up at the group demands great courage. But we're worth it. Our child is worth it.

We want to do this well. We want to grieve in healthy ways that bring honor to the child we lost and empower us to love those around us. Other grieving parents can help. We must find each other. We need each other badly.

Affirmation: I will find other grieving parents who can support me during this time. I need people who get it, who understand. Over time, perhaps I can support others.

I FEEL STRANGE

FROM THE GRIEVING HEART:

My grief feels different from what I imagined.

I knew someone who had lost a child. I tried to imagine what it was like for them. I couldn't get there.

I didn't want to think about it. It was too painful and terrifying. I forced the thought out of my mind.

Now, here I am, enduring the loss of you. I can say this for certain: my grief is not what I would have expected. It's deeper and more painful than I could have possibly imagined.

There's also a sort of mysterious richness to my grief. I think it comes from love and gratitude. I love you. I'm so grateful for you. You were such a gift to me.

You, my child, played a massive role in who I have become. So, there is a sense in which you're never very far away. You're a part of me. You're right here, inside me.

I see you when I look in the mirror, as weird as that sounds. I hear you in my words and tone of voice. I feel you in my gestures. You're everywhere, all the time.

Of course, what I mostly feel is the emptiness of you not being here. Your presence was so large and powerful in my life. I'm still not ready to accept a world without you.

My grief is a mix of stunned disbelief, painful emptiness, and rich love and gratitude all at the same time.

Strange.

It's all so strange. Your not being here is strange. I feel strange.

I miss you. I wish I could see you. I wish we could talk. I could use a hug, too.

"Strange."

This is a word often used to describe grief in general, and especially the process of working through the loss of a child. Everything seems weird and surreal.

A stabbing pain attacks and moves us to scream and wail. A stunned sense of shock paralyzes our minds and hearts at times. Love and gratitude well up within us. We cry and laugh at the same memories. Grieving the departure of a child is indeed a mixed bag of strangeness.

Most things in our life are reduced to checklists. We order our days and check things off as we go along. We somehow naturally expect grief to be predictable and manageable somehow. At least, that's what we thought before we lost our child.

Grief, however, defies our attempts to stuff it into a to-do list. We quickly discover that grieving the loss of a son or daughter is a dynamic, back-and-forth, up-and-down process where progress is difficult to measure at times.

In fact, sometimes we don't want to "progress." We want to go back. We want our child with us. Adjustment and recovery can seem like an insult to the sacredness of our parent-child bond. Movement forward seems like we're distancing ourselves from our son or daughter, and we want none of that.

Grief refuses to be mastered. It is a matter of the heart. It is a season to be lived through.

Just as we have no control over the seasons, so we don't have reins on grief either. When a new season arrives, we adjust our lifestyle to navigate it well and in healthy ways.

The loss of a child requires massive adjustment. The adjustments are emotional, mental, physical, spiritual, and relational. Nothing escapes unaffected. Being patient with ourselves is important.

Perhaps it's time to dump our expectations of what we think this grief should be like and what life will be now. Our hearts need to feel this through and express themselves.

For now, we focus on taking our hearts seriously and expressing our grief in responsible and healthy ways. We accept that our grief is a process that will not be boxed or controlled. As much as possible, we live in the moment.

Yes, this season feels strange, and that's okay. Life is different now.

Affirmation: This season of grief will feel strange at times. That's okay because life is different now.

FOR REFLECTION AND/OR JOURNALING

MY GRIEVING HEART:

"I wonder if losing you is affecting my body and my physical health. For example, I notice that…"

I MISS YOUR VOICE

FROM THE GRIEVING HEART:

I miss your voice.

I watched a few videos last night. It was wonderful and awful at the same time. I was thrilled to hear your voice, but the tears started flowing immediately.

I watched them again. And again. I closed my eyes and could almost see you. I kept them closed for a long time, my imagination basking in your presence.

Yes, I miss your voice. I miss you.

Since then, I've listened differently. I'm paying attention to the voices around me. I'm more present somehow. Our voices have such power. They come from within and are so personal and individual.

I miss your words, your laughter, and your singing. I can hear you in my heart - your voice at different stages of your life. I watched the videos again. Pain and longing speared my heart.

It feels like a thousand needles have been thrust into my soul. What is this world I'm in – without you in it?

The human voice has great power. We use it to express our minds, hearts, love, and angst. Our voice identifies us. When we hear the voice of someone we love, we smile.

When a child dies, we naturally miss their voice. We miss the interaction and connection. We miss their physical presence and everything else associated with their voice. We remember past words, phrases, and conversations.

If we're fortunate, we have voicemails and videos of our child. We listen, and their voice triggers all the emotions churning deep within us. For a moment, we're with them again. Perhaps we can even feel their presence.

With their voice, they spoke to us. They shared themselves with us. They laughed and sang. They told us they cared about and loved us. Their words filtered into our hearts and souls. Their voice became a part of us.

Right now, listening to their voice might bring pain and sadness. There will come a day when hearing the same message or watching the same video will bring laughter and joy. For now, we simply let the grief come. Our tears and sadness honor them. Our grief is one way we say, "I love you."

Affirmation: I miss you and long to hear your voice. I love you.

YOUR BIRTHDAY IS COMING UP

FROM THE GRIEVING HEART:

Your birthday is coming up. What do I do with that?

I want to remember you somehow, but I'm honestly dreading the pain that I know will come.

I must bear the pain. I love you. I will remember and find ways to grieve well.

I'm so glad you were born. I remember the day you were born. It was magical. Yes, parts of it were hard, but once you arrived, my heart was filled with a love I didn't know was possible.

A special love. A different sort of love. The love of a parent for a child.

I held you. You were mine. I knew you were one-of-a-kind. No one and nothing could match you.

Amazing. Wonderful. Special.

Why did you have to go? The pain of all this grief is intense. I feel like I'm dying inside, slowly, day by day. How can I live on with you not here?

Yet, I must. I will live and honor you. I will live, and live well, as you would want me to.

I took so much for granted. Does it take a death to appreciate what life truly means?

I feel guilty about taking anything for granted – your presence,

your voice, your laughter, your physical existence in this world.
Now my heart is cracked and broken, and my soul is leaking out.

I will face your birthday and express my love for
you. I will remember and honor you.

It will be hard, but I will make it good somehow. You deserve that.

Birthdays used to be times of celebration. Once a son or daughter departs, their birthday becomes a massive grief trigger. We remember, and memories can be painful. We look at the calendar with dread, wondering how we're going to make it through this special day.

Some hunker down, close the blinds, turn off the lights, and hibernate. Others take time to remember and whisper words of thanks or gratitude. Still others make specific plans to honor their child on their birthday. These plans can include presents, letters, cards, a special event, a donation, or serving in their name in a cause that was important to them. Some light a candle or set up an empty chair in remembrance. Many share this special occasion on social media and invite others to express memories.

This special day will be difficult for us. It will be emotional. We might have painful or even disturbing memories. All this is a natural part of the grief process.

Our child's birthday will come, and keep coming, every year. We will fare better if we can make a simple plan for the day. Just the act of being proactive can unplug some of our dread. We can honor them, grieve well, and make the day count.

This is part of loving them, even after they're gone.

Affirmation: I will be proactive and make a simple plan for your birthday. I will honor you and express my love.

I FEEL TRAPPED SOMETIMES

FROM THE GRIEVING HEART:

I was doing fine yesterday. At least I thought I was.

I was driving along, not paying much attention. I found myself stopped at a red light and looked to the right. I saw something that reminded me of you. I lost it.

I had to pull over into the closest parking lot. I sat there and sobbed. Someone knocked on my window and asked if I was alright. I felt like a fool.

My grief is like that. It can make a fool out of me without warning. No way to prepare for it. No way to anticipate it. Every moment, I'm at the mercy of my surroundings and my emotions.

I wiped my face, started the car, and drove off. I had to pull over three more times before I got home. I sat in the driveway for what felt like an hour. I was in shock again. Stunned and paralyzed.

I go around and around in a circle. The same emotions cycle back, again and again. I feel trapped sometimes.

Perhaps this is all just my heart looking for you. I don't know. It's confusing and sad. It hurts.

As we quickly discover, grief bursts can descend upon us anytime, anywhere. Anything can trigger a memory and release the thoughts and feelings associated with it. These sudden grief spikes can feel like an invasion, an assault on our peace of mind and heart.

Though grief bursts can seem random and unpredictable, we can be proactive in how we deal with them. First, we need to accept that these bursts of emotion will come. They are natural, common, and inevitable. They can vary greatly in length and intensity. The grief is within us, and it slowly builds up over time. Along comes a trigger, and a sudden pressure release occurs.

Again, this is a natural, common, and healthy process. When a grief burst comes, we can acknowledge the emotion we feel. We give ourselves permission to grieve. If we're unable to express our grief at that moment, we can make a simple plan for when and where we will. Many times, it can simply mean excusing ourselves and heading somewhere close by that's more private.

We loved, and so we grieve. Our grief bursts honor our child. By planning ahead, we can learn to handle them with increased confidence and peace.

Our hearts are expressing themselves. We miss our child. We're grieving.

Affirmation: I will be proactive and plan for how I will handle the grief bursts that come.

YOU ARE STILL PART OF THIS FAMILY

FROM THE GRIEVING HEART:

You are still a part of this family.

I don't care what happened or how or when. I don't care how old you were. I don't care what anyone else thinks or says. You might be gone, but you're still here too. You live on in us.

We're so rich for having known you. You are unique, special, priceless. You are a part of us. You always will be.

So, we're going to live that way. I'm going to live that way, and others can come along if they want to.

I'll find a way to include you in things. In special times. In holiday events. In family gatherings and celebrations. Not talking about you isn't going to help. Remembering you and being honest with our own hearts might be emotional, but I don't know how it can't be good.

We still love you. We must find ways to express that. I must find ways to express that, and often.

I want you to be a part of my everyday life. I want to think about you, talk about you, and even talk to you. You occupy a special place in my heart, and your death doesn't change that.

In fact, your death makes that special place inside me, well, all the more special.

Yes, you're still a part of this family. We are yours, and you are ours.

My child, I love you.

After the loss of our child, we live in a new and strange world. They are no longer physically present, yet they are as much a part of us as ever. We can't hug or kiss them, but we can embrace them fondly in our hearts. We can't call, text, or email them, but we can share as if they're right here with us - because they are, in our hearts.

Our children occupy some very special real estate in our hearts and souls. When a child dies, they don't cease to exist within us. The memories are full, rich, and powerful. Our child is an essential part of us and our families, and always will be.

Yes, certain things will fade with time. This is natural and normal. But we can intentionally carry our kids with us, in healthy ways. We can choose to remember and honor them in significant ways. We can deliberately include them in special times, on holidays, and at family gatherings. As families, we can help each other grieve, heal, and grow by expressing what we miss and are thankful for.

Our child may not be physically present, but when we intentionally include them in the family going forward, we give ourselves a chance to live more fully from our hearts. Otherwise, there is this important and essential part of us, the heart-space occupied by our child, that gets hidden or neglected.

We want to live well. Our child would want that. That means living from our hearts with love, meaning, and purpose. That's going to require that we take our child with us on the adventure ahead. They were a key part of our past. They deserve their place in our present and future too.

Affirmation: You'll always be part of me and of our family. I'll do what I can to make sure we remember you and take you with us.

CAN'T THEY SEE I'M HURTING?

FROM THE GRIEVING HEART:

My heart is already broken. Why do the people around me have to crush and shatter what's left of it? Can't they see I'm hurting? Don't they care?

"Life goes on, and you need to move on." I have heard this lovely, encouraging sentiment more times and in more ways than I can count. It's a knife to my soul, a blow to my gut, every time.

Yes, life goes on. Of course. But my world has changed. You're not in it, and that affects everything. My life feels like it's on pause, while everyone else appears to be speeding along unaffected.

Time is moving on, yes. But I'm not sure I am. And if moving on means leaving you behind, forget it.

I know I need to say goodbye. I've said goodbye to you many times already. Something deep inside me screams and aches. I miss you. I would rather say hello.

Though you're gone, I know that you're always with me. You're part of me. I carry you in my heart.

Life goes on, and I am learning to go on without your physical presence.

But I don't like it. Not one bit.

Yes, well-meaning people can say some unhelpful and insensitive things. Perhaps there are times when what's said is even calculated to hurt. People get frustrated with our grief because it reminds them of their losses. When we show up, it's a reminder that some children die before their parents, and that terrifies them. Rather than dealing with their own pain and fears, they shove them back down inside and dole out curt advice to us instead.

Life moves on. Life is always moving. Time marches forward. But when we lose a child, our hearts are stunned and even paralyzed for a time. For all practical purposes, time stops for us. Our world abruptly halts. We move in a daze. We go through the motions, doing what needs to be done, but our hearts and souls are elsewhere.

Grief is necessary. It is a natural and normal response to a loss. It is nature's way of healing a shattered soul. We live in a new world now, without the physical presence of our son or daughter. Their absence hovers over us and colors everything. Recovery, whatever that means for each of us, takes time.

As we walk this unpredictable, rocky road of grief, we remember our child and find ways to honor them. We discover, one step at a time, how to take them with us as we walk life's new, yet untraveled pathways. We say goodbye in some ways, but we never leave them behind. They are part of us in many ways.

And we never forget. We can't. We love them.

Affirmation: I will engage in life today as best as I can, remembering you.

FOR REFLECTION AND/OR JOURNALING

MY GRIEVING HEART:

"When sudden grief bursts come, I can deal with them by…"

WHERE HAVE ALL THE LISTENERS GONE?

FROM THE GRIEVING HEART:

I can't do this alone. I don't want to do this alone.

Yet, I feel so lonely.

No one seems to understand. I guess that's reasonable. No one can see inside my heart, read my mind, or feel my emotions. But I want someone to understand. I need to be seen, heard, and understood.

Maybe being seen and heard would be enough.
That would be a great start, in any case.

Where do I find the people I need? Where have all the listeners gone? I know everyone is busy with their own lives and that meeting me where I am is going to require patience and energy.

I have figured out that if a person hasn't experienced significant loss, and especially the loss of a child, they can't have a hope of being with me in this. They simply can't get there.

And even if they've lost a child, they're not me and they didn't lose you. No wonder I feel lonely.

I need someone who knows grief. I need someone like me.

Grief is a lonely road, but we were never meant to travel it alone. Loss is a universal experience. We all have people we care about leave, disappear, or die. Many of us are walking this demanding, unpredictable path. Finding fellow travelers can be a key to adjusting and living with loss.

We all need to be seen and heard, especially when we're hurting. Usually, people who know grief – especially those who have lost children - are the ones who can see and relate to us the best. These people look into our eyes and sense our pain. They've been on this road. They know what it has been like for them, and they can better imagine what it might be like for us. They can do better than sympathize. They can empathize.

Yes, some fellow grievers are fixers and advice-givers. Some will compare their losses with ours and decide whose is worse or more difficult. Others, however, understand that there is no fixing this. They enter our lives with no agenda. On some level, they feel our pain and know that the best thing they can do is simply be with us. They offer us their presence.

Some are fortunate enough to have these people in their own families. Others find supportive fellow grievers in support groups, at church, or in a civic organization. Some feel safe and heard in online groups and forums. Grief counselors or spiritual mentors can also be a huge help.

We need others who know grief, and they need us. We're in this together.

Affirmation: I will find people who will listen
and walk this grief road with me.

GUILT CAME VISITING AGAIN

FROM THE GRIEVING HEART:

Today guilt came visiting again. I can't seem to shake it.

I get better for a while, and then a cloud descends. I feel responsible somehow. After all, I'm your parent. Doesn't this come back and fall on me, somehow, some way?

Surely, I could have protected you somehow. I should have said or done something more. I should have seen this or that coming.

I have deep regrets. I have memories I wish I could forget.

Is this just me trying to hold on to you somehow? Am I wanting to feel responsible? Is this my heart working overtime to make sense out of you leaving?

Yes, I feel guilty. There's a constant, dull pressure on my chest. I want to lay blame somewhere. I admit that guilt feels good sometimes. It gives my emotion a target, someplace to go.

All of this seems so big, and I feel so small. It's all above my pay grade and way beyond my abilities to resolve. I wish my heart would heal and be more at peace. I feel so unsteady and shaky right now.

In the end, I know feeling guilty doesn't help. It won't bring you back. Nothing will. Does anyone else feel this way?

Guilt often hides in the recesses of our hearts and pops up at the most inconvenient times. We think we've resolved things. We seem to have let go a little and forgiven ourselves for whatever we might have done or said, not done or not said. Then we wake up and find guilt hanging out in our living room. It smiles and begins its accusations all over again.

"You're their parent. You should have known. How could you let this happen?"

We said before that guilt will come knocking, repetitively. We can refuse to answer, but we can't stop it from making noise. It sneaks in when we're not aware. Before we know it, we're thinking those guilty, it's-all-my-fault thoughts again.

We could get discouraged with ourselves. We could get angry and swear that we'll never feel guilty again. We could venture down darker roads, assuming responsibility that isn't ours and wondering what punishment might fit us the best.

On the other hand, we can remind ourselves that this is the nature of guilt — it keeps knocking and popping up, again and again. When it comes, we can acknowledge this unwanted visitor and then release it. Release, release, and release again, as many times as necessary.

The grief of losing a child is heavy enough without guilt attached to it. We breathe deeply. We tell ourselves that guilt's voice is not our own. We see guilt as the foreign invader it is and forgive ourselves yet again.

Affirmation: I'll release guilt and forgive myself as many times as necessary. This grief is heavy enough without allowing guilt to become my constant companion.

I'M IN CONTROL OF SO LITTLE

FROM THE GRIEVING HEART:

Yesterday, it was guilt. Today, it's anger. I'm back at it again. Surely someone somewhere is responsible for all this.

In the end, my mind figures that all the possible roads of blame end with God. At the end of the day, he's responsible, right? And yet, if he is good, how can he be responsible for tragedies, disasters, and evil? But if he is in control, then how is he not ultimately responsible for the pain and suffering in the world?

Your leaving has generated all kinds of questions, seemingly unsolvable riddles, and uncomfortable wonderings. I don't know how strong my faith was before all this, but now it feels shaky.

I guess that's not surprising since I feel shaky. My whole world seems to be tottering. I'm surrounded by people, but I feel so alone.

Perhaps no one is to blame. Maybe it's all coincidence and random. What about chance or fate? I don't know.

I can't believe that you being my child is random and simply by chance. That makes our relationship an accident. That scares me more than all the other options.

One thing is certain. I'm in control of very little, and that's unnerving. I feel that I am at the whim of forces much greater than myself, and I don't know what to do with that.

I feel small. Insignificant. Helpless.

The loss of a child can create spiritual questioning. This is natural and common. Our world has been upended, and whatever we believed about life, ourselves, the universe, and God may be undergoing an intense examination in our hearts and minds. If what we think or believe doesn't provide sufficient answers for what happened, we might be thrown into a crisis of faith.

The pain of missing our son or daughter can be so intense that we find ourselves wondering what we believe deep down inside where no one else can see. Most of us seek answers that will allow us to be more at peace with ourselves, with what happened, and with the world around us. Many of us are extremely uncomfortable with the unknown. We see mysteries as something to be solved and revealed, and not as unknowns to be lived with.

We hunger to know. We long to understand. But most of all, we hurt, because we dared to love.

Yes, we know that the mortality rate among humans is 100%. But we were supposed to go first. The death of our child is out-of-order. It feels all wrong somehow. When a son or daughter takes their last breath, the shocking reality of their departure comes crashing in on us and we are undone by the power of child loss.

At the end of the day, we are all human. Our hearts are resilient, yet incredibly fragile. We're wired for connection, and our children are some of the deepest attachments our hearts make. When this strand of our life-web is severed, everything shakes.

Our hearts and souls search for answers. We look for our child, even though we know they're gone.

Affirmation: What I believe might be shaken or undergo some intense examination. This is natural.

WHAT DOES IT MATTER?

FROM THE GRIEVING HEART:

On some days, like today, I don't want to do anything.

I'm drained. Exhausted. Life feels so heavy. Nothing seems to matter much. I find myself asking, "So what?"

What does it matter if I get up today and do what I'm supposed to do? Who cares?

We chase after possessions and prestige. We climb whatever ladder is set in front of us, struggling and competing to get to the top. And then what? Ultimately, we die. And we may lose anything and everything along the way.

Life seems pointless at times. Maybe my heart is waving the white flag, ready to surrender the battle of trying to make sense of your leaving and this new, unwanted life I find myself in.

I don't enjoy what I used to. All is dull and drab. I have no motivation. I'm a big ball of do-nothing and go-nowhere. I'm in a hole, and I want to crawl in deeper.

Apathetic. That's what I am. Am I going downhill here? Is this temporary? Can I get out of this hole? Will I want to?

Too many questions. No wonder I'm exhausted.

I wish you were here.

The loss of a child can suck us dry. When we feel drained and exhausted, apathy is often not far behind. We simply don't have the energy to care.

All our resources have been shifted into survival gear. Our systems are focused on maintaining enough equilibrium that we can adjust, recover, and eventually heal over time. Our batteries have automatically switched into energy-saving mode.

No wonder we're not as motivated. It's enough of a battle to keep going and doing life from day to day without our child. Periods of loss and heavy emotion are typically not a time for making big decisions and trying to move ahead. This season is one of grief. And grief is necessary to process and heal from a loss, especially the loss of a daughter or son.

At some point, it's healthy if we consider and alter our expectations of ourselves to fit where we are. Our main agenda is to guard our hearts and grieve in as healthy a way as possible. This honors our child and our relationship with them. All else is secondary. As we grieve well, the rest of life will fall into place over time.

For now, the goal is to be patient with ourselves, others, and our current routine. We might feel pointless, meaningless, and apathetic. We might feel like we're stuck in a pit with no way out. As we grieve, this will change.

Thankfully, now is not forever.

Affirmation: Even if I feel empty and apathetic, I'll be patient with myself. I trust that this will change over time.

I FEEL DEPRESSED

FROM THE GRIEVING HEART:

I feel depressed. No wonder. Life is depressing right now.

I'm not myself. I used to smile. Now, smiling is just a show, a facade. I'm beginning to tire of this counterfeit lifestyle I seem to be living in public. Performing and holding it together for everyone else takes way too much energy.

There are times I want to bust out, forget what's acceptable, and shout how I really feel about all this.

"How are you?" people ask. "Well, I'm not fine. I'm angry, frustrated, and hurt. I'm sad, depressed, and lonely. I'm confused, anxious, and afraid. I'm grieving."

It would feel so good to say that. Why can't I?

I guess I think it would only make things worse. I'm already being treated like I have an infectious disease. People avoid me. It's obvious they don't know what to do with me. Honestly, I don't know what to do with myself either.

So, I hide. I keep it inside. No wonder I feel depressed.

How could I not feel depressed? You're not here.

After the loss of a child, feeling depressed is natural and common. When a daughter or son departs, the effects can be devastating. Our hearts are feeling the extent of this terrible, unthinkable loss.

We're tired, even exhausted. Our emotions are heavy and oppressive. We don't feel like ourselves. We can't function as we've become accustomed to. Putting one foot in front of the other takes more out of us than we would have ever dreamed.

We look at the past and long for it. We look ahead, and all is hazy. We've had other losses, but we've never been here before. Everything has changed now. Feeling depressed is a natural response for a shattered heart.

Perhaps we can find a little relief if we remember that most depression in grief is temporary and situational. It's not where we were or where we will be, but it's where we are now. This is part of love.

We feel our child's absence. It hurts. Our hearts crack. Our bodies feel the tumultuous onslaught of our grief. Our souls are hit with the pain.

Accepting ourselves, even when depressed, is important. Others may not understand, which makes it even more crucial to give ourselves a break.

We are where we are. As we grieve, our emotions will change over time.

Affirmation: I will accept myself and trust that any depression I experience is temporary and will pass with time.

FOR REFLECTION AND/OR JOURNALING

MY GRIEVING HEART:

"As I learn to live without your physical presence, some ways that I can express my love and honor you are..."

I MISS EVERYTHING

FROM THE GRIEVING HEART:

I miss you.

I miss your voice, your presence, and your laughter.
I miss your smile, your eyes, and your hugs.

I miss everything. I love you.

I wonder if this intense sadness, this depression
I'm experiencing, will ever get better.

What if it goes on and on? What if I don't feel better?
What if all this gets the better of me and I end up
living as a shell of a person for the rest of my life?

What if this pit I'm in becomes my home? What if
the depression stays, and becomes my life?

Just the thought of it is terrifying. Life looks so dark and dreary. It's
hard to imagine this cloud lifting. I've forgotten what joy feels like.

I don't like this. Missing you is worse than I could
have ever dreamed. In fact, my life is becoming
a perpetual nightmare without you.

I want to be out of this pit and feel the sunlight and breeze
on my face again. I want to live. Have I forgotten how?

In grief, it is common for us to assume that the way things are now is how they will be in the future. We can see the past, but our future has been altered and disrupted. If we're experiencing depression, we naturally wonder how long this will continue.

Is this grief more than for a season? Is this our new life? Will we be able to get out of this pit?

If our depression deepens to the point where we don't go out, don't get out of bed, and don't function in daily life, it's possible that something more than temporary situational depression is at work. This isn't only about the loss of our child, but it is also influenced by our current situation, including our physical condition, financial stability, relational support network, and overall mental and emotional health. Other recent losses or major life changes can also complicate things.

If we become isolated and non-functional for two weeks or more, it's time to reach out and seek professional help. Grief counselors, therapists, physicians, and clergy are often sought for their expertise during these times. If we're having suicidal thoughts, the temptation is to keep this to ourselves. This is the last thing we should do. If self-harm is part of our thought life, it's best to call 911 or seek help immediately.

There is no shame in seeking help. Reaching out is wise and is part of taking our own hearts seriously.

Affirmation: I miss everything about you. If my depression deepens, I'll reach out for help. This is part of loving myself, and you.

If you're having thoughts of harming or killing yourself, please reach out now.

National Suicide Hotline
1-800-273-8255 (1-800-273-TALK)
Crisis Text Line
Text "home" to 741741

WHY DO PEOPLE SAY SUCH THINGS?

FROM THE GRIEVING HEART:

Why do people feel like they have to compare? It seems like everyone wants to compare their losses to mine.

"My mom passed away ten years ago, so I know how you feel."

"I lost a friend in high school, and it was much worse than this."

"You think you're hurting? I've lost five people in the last two years."

"You think this is bad? It only gets worse."

Why do people say such things? All people are not the same. Every relationship is different. Even if they lost a child, they didn't lose you. They can't see and know my heart or my pain. What do they know?

We all need to express our grief. I get that. But why do we have to play the comparison game while we grieve?

As human beings, we tend to compare. We wonder how we're doing, or how we're supposed to be doing, so we look around and evaluate. When we start to compare emotional pain, however, we're in dangerous territory.

Grieving hearts don't need to be evaluated, but rather they long to be seen and heard. We need connection, not comparison. When others make our pain about them and their grief, we naturally feel invisible or even belittled.

It would be nice if we could meet each other where we are and express kindness. Honestly, listening and expressing compassion is often easier than living a self-focused, self-centered life. Our hearts long for mutual relationships. Having someone thrust themselves upon us is a boundary violation that does not sit well with our souls.

Words matter. Words can hurt. And yet, we can't afford to let unfeeling statements of comparison rule our minds and hearts. If we're willing, we can use unhelpful statements like those above as fuel for our grief fire. We can find ways to process our emotions about these encounters in ways that allow us to empty a little bit of our grief reservoir.

Comparison never benefits anyone. It can steal our identity and keep joy far from us.

Affirmation: I'll find ways to express my grief
without comparing my loss to that of others.
Comparison does not help me grieve well.

I DON'T LIKE THIS NEW LIFE

FROM THE GRIEVING HEART:

I don't like this new life. I want a life with you back in it. I miss talking to you. I want to hear your voice — not a voicemail, but your real voice. I want you here, now.

I get so frustrated I want to scream. Yesterday, I did. I didn't even realize it. I let it rip. It felt so good, I screamed again, this time into my pillow. That felt good too, but not nearly as satisfying as letting it fill the air, full force.

I have so much inside me. I think it builds up over time. That makes sense. I hide so much just to be able to be around people and get through the day. I stuff more than I realize. I need a pressure release from time to time and screaming seems to fit the bill.

I can feel the emotion welling up inside, moving from my torso and up into my throat. I've been slamming the door shut on it since you left. No more. I'm going to scream. If I'm around people, I'll excuse myself and head to the car. I'm betting the car would make a good screaming place.

My heart has a huge hole in it. You're worth screaming about.

Life was already crazy. With you gone, it's even more nuts. When I think about screaming, I smile.

Smiling feels good.

Finding healthy ways to grieve while remaining functional can be challenging. When our child departed, all the rules of life changed somehow. We all do life in teams, and our team is not the same anymore.

For most, it's natural to want to hole up and grieve quietly on our own. As time goes by, the grief inside begins to build up. Our internal grief reservoir rises. Sooner or later, we need space to allow it to overflow.

Many grieving the loss of a child find screaming to be a great way to release pent-up tension and emotion. Some scream into pillows. Some scream in their cars. I know a swimmer who screams underwater in the pool. Expressing the powerful emotions in short bursts can be effective and relieving. Periodically, we need to air what's inside.

Grief will be expressed, one way or another. Better to let it out in healthy ways than to force it to leak out in ways we might later regret.

Some things are worth screaming about. The loss of a child is certainly one of those.

Affirmation: Life is tough and losing you is painful. There's plenty to scream about.

I'M MISSING THE FUTURE

FROM THE GRIEVING HEART:

I have been missing the past. Now, I'm missing the future.

I'm missing my future with you in it. You won't be there. You won't be here on your birthday. Or my birthday. You'll be absent at Thanksgiving, Christmas, and every other holiday. Every special day we had will now consist of those of us left behind and our memories of you.

I've not only lost you, but I've also lost the future I was anticipating. Everything is different, and so is the future.

I thought I knew who I was, what I was doing, and where I was going. Now, I'm not so sure. Every thought and picture I had of the future had you in it. Now there is only empty space where you would have been.

Sounds strange to say I need to grieve a lost future. Yet, that's reality. I miss what I had. I miss what I anticipated. I miss you.

I know I will somehow make it through this, but I don't like it at all.

When a daughter or son departs, our world changes, and that includes the future. What we anticipated will be significantly altered. Part of what we planned on will be no more. Our lives will be deeply affected going forward.

When hit by this devastating loss, we not only grieve what we had but also what we will not have in the future. Unfortunately, along the way we discover other losses that are also connected to our child – relationships, activities, holidays, traditions, hopes, dreams, and plans. It's never about just the one loss but includes all the other strands of our life-web.

Life is about relationships. When a son or daughter exits, the future we had envisioned changes. With each holiday or special event, we become hyper-aware of their absence. Our grief surfaces, and powerful emotions can hijack us at a moment's notice.

Our hearts are shattered. The future seems uncertain and hazy now. Though it might be hard to believe, the future can can still be good. We can help make it good by taking our hearts seriously and grieving well.

Of course, we miss them and wish they were here. We can't imagine the road ahead without them. That's okay. The answers we need will come when our hearts are ready for them.

Affirmation: It's hard to imagine a future without you in it. I will focus on grieving well and celebrating you along the way.

I'M TIRED OF GRIEF

FROM THE GRIEVING HEART:

I don't like the looks I'm getting. Maybe I'm being too sensitive or seeing what's not there, but it feels like people are tired of me and my grief.

I'm tired of my grief too, but it's not like I can wish it away. The emotions rattle inside me, like some ricocheting superball – back and forth, up and down. I'm exhausted. I can't think, and yet my mind is spinning. I sleep but can't seem to rest.

Yes, I'm tired of grief. I'm tired, period.

I know that being with someone who's grieving is not the easiest thing in the world. Perhaps it's frustrating and draining. If so, no wonder people don't want to be around me. They all just want me to feel better.

I get that. I want me to feel better too. I wish I could.

But right now, I hurt. I can't seem to hide it, either. My grief spills out, unbidden and unwanted.

I'm still a mess. Will any of this ever get any better?

Grief can wear us out. After a while, our energy reserves begin to be depleted. Our ability and desire to hold our grief in check may dwindle. Sadness, anger, and frustration begin to ooze out of our pores and onto the world around us.

People who love us are naturally concerned. It's hard for us and difficult for them. Watching us hurt and suffer isn't easy for them, but it's where we are at the moment.

Being able to accept another person for where they are at any given time is both a gift and a skill. Some people seem to do this naturally and almost effortlessly. Others grow so uncomfortable with grief and its emotions that they either try to pull us out of where we are or distance themselves from us. It's a challenging place to be, for everyone.

And it's especially difficult for those of us with hearts shattered from the loss of a daughter or son.

We want to feel better. We wish we could. Some days are okay. Others are dark and painful. Getting through the day can require all we've got.

The best we can do is be ourselves, as much as possible. We grieve and let the chips fall where they may. Others' responses are their own. It's not our job to take care of those around us emotionally. They must do that for themselves.

We breathe deeply, forgive quickly, and grieve.

Affirmation: I can't control the words and actions of others. I'll focus on grieving and being the best me possible in this situation.

FOR REFLECTION AND/OR JOURNALING

MY GRIEVING HEART:

"So far, here are some things I'm learning on this grief journey:"

I HOPE THIS GETS BETTER, EVENTUALLY

FROM THE GRIEVING HEART:

People seem shy around me. And no one mentions you. Why is that?

Are they worried about upsetting me? I'm already upset.

Are they concerned about me getting emotional? Don't they know I'm already grieving and can't help it?

Do they not want me to think about you? Don't they know you're always in my heart and never far from my mind?

Have they forgotten you? Don't they know I can't?

They may not talk about you, but I will. I will speak your name. I will say it out loud and often – a hundred times in a row if I want.

You are the invisible elephant in every room. Why can't we talk about you? Why can't we share what we miss and what you meant to us? Why can't we grieve together?

Maybe I'm unrealistic. Perhaps this is simply the way the world works. Even children die, depart, and life goes on. I know they didn't lose you – and some of them didn't even know you. I can't expect them to get it or understand.

It would be nice if they were sensitive and mentioned you from time to time, but that's up to them.

Grief is lonely.

I hope this gets better, eventually.

There might be people who mention our child. Some who knew them might even share what they miss about them, but chances are these people will be few. Most will express sympathy at first, and then promptly go on with their lives.

We're stunned, immobilized, and trying to figure out what happened, why, and what it means. It's as if we relocated to a new life. The world looks familiar, yet everything has changed. Our child is gone and all of life feels different. It would be nice if others accepted this, but we certainly can't expect them to understand it.

We can't wait around for others to mention our child and ask about them. We must take our own hearts seriously and begin speaking their names as often and as loudly as we need to.

We courageously share stories and memories with others. We encourage others who knew them to mention our child and share with us what they miss about them.

As we bravely speak their names, we give ourselves and others a chance to grieve. We present others with an invitation to join us in our grief. It might be emotionally uncomfortable, but it can be good and healing. Perhaps some will distance themselves, and that's okay. We must grieve. It's where we are.

We will speak their names. Often.

Affirmation: Even if others don't mention you, I will. I'll give us a chance to grieve together.

SILENCE, LISTENING EARS, AND A HUG CAN DO WONDERS

FROM THE GRIEVING HEART:

Yesterday a good friend said, "Well, at least you had them as long as you did. You were blessed."

Yes, I'm blessed. But I wanted you longer. Much longer.

It reminds me of another statement last week, when a co-worker hugged me and stated, "At least they're in a better place now."

I agree, but I want you here, now.

Anything beginning with "At least…" is void of any comfort to me at all.

I'm ashamed to remember that I've used my share of "At least…" statements in the past. "At least they're not suffering anymore." "At least you had a wonderful relationship." "At least you have a good, supportive family."

I didn't know what to say. I guess I thought I had to say something. I know better now.

A little silence, listening ears, and a hug can do wonders.

When someone experiences the loss of a child, no one knows what to say. There are no words for such things. All verbal attempts to fix, encourage, or somehow make things better fall to the ground with little or no fruit.

We've all been recipients of some at-least statements. Though some of these might be true, few are comforting. Grieving hearts need to be seen, heard, and understood, and these statements come across more as platitudes. We spout them off without thinking how the grieving heart in front of us might hear it.

Yes, these statements will come. People don't know what to say, so they tend to say what they've heard in similar situations. Of course, we would be better served if those around us spent less time talking and more time listening to our hearts and souls. Though it sounds simple, this requires time, patience, and a willingness to be in the presence of emotional suffering. In our world, convenience is king, and there is nothing convenient about loss and grief.

We all need to be seen and heard. People who are acquainted with grief and with whom we feel safe are our best bet. And if we've said things we now regret to other grieving hearts in the past, it's time to forgive ourselves. We're now in a different place. Now we know this pain, and we're much better equipped to engage with and comfort other grieving hearts.

A little silence, listening ears, and a hug can indeed do wonders. Our hearts heal moment by moment and piece by piece when we give to others what we ourselves need.

Affirmation: Since I now know grief, I can engage with other grieving hearts. This will be healing and comforting for me as well.

I HAD NO IDEA

FROM THE GRIEVING HEART:

I've been thinking more about my responses in the past when I encountered those who were grieving. I feel sad about my lack of compassion. I didn't know. I couldn't have known.

Until I lost you, I had no idea what this kind of pain was like. I thought I could imagine a bit, and maybe put myself in others' shoes. Now, I know such thinking is arrogant. How could I know without having been there?

When others lost loved ones, I was sympathetic for a while. But honestly, I expected them to be back to normal quickly. And I expected them to be the same people they were before.

Ridiculous.

Losing you has broken my heart. Now, I can recognize other broken hearts. Loss and grief have made life more real and each day more important. For these things, I'm grateful.

There are many grieving hearts out there, more than I could ever know.

Until we encounter significant loss, we tend to be quick to judge. We march along our daily routine, comparing ourselves with others. We always come out ahead or short. We evaluate others and ourselves. Above all, we avoid being uncomfortable. Loss, grief, and the accompanying emotions can be unnerving.

Now that we know the terrible, heavy loss of a daughter or son, our hearts are more sensitive. We know what brokenness and the loneliness of loss feel like. We can now empathize as well as sympathize. We can bring comfort to other grieving hearts because we know grief.

Some of us might like our alone time, but no one enjoys feeling alone. We're wired for relationship and hunger for connection more than most of us realize. Grief might separate us from some people we've known, but it can also connect us to others. These new connections can be deep and meaningful.

Grieving is hard, exhausting work. Every day can be a battle. We need comrades for this fight — people we can trust and count on. We can be those people for other grieving hearts, if we're willing. We can be comforters, even while hurting. And this can bring a new sense of meaning to our pain and suffering.

We're in this together, and we need each other — badly.

Affirmation: Even though I'm hurting, I can comfort others. My pain has purpose.

GET OVER YOU? IMPOSSIBLE.

FROM THE GRIEVING HEART:

My own family doesn't understand. I thought that they, of all people, would be compassionate and helpful.

Don't get me wrong. Some relatives have been great. They're not me, and so they don't understand entirely, but they're respectful. They don't evaluate how I'm doing or try to fix me. They simply love me where I am.

Others, however, are sending the message, "Aren't you over this by now? Buck up."

Get over you? Impossible.

The fact that this comes from family hurts even more. Family members are supposed to be safe, right? I guess people are, well, people. We seem to be basically selfish and most interested in what's comfortable and pleasant for us. But it's still disappointing.

I'm grateful for supportive relatives. I can entrust my heart and emotions to them. With the others, I'll guard my heart and try to extend the understanding and compassion to them that they seem unable to give me.

I will not let unkind responses take control of or overly influence my heart.

You are my child. We had a unique relationship. My grief is unique too. The loneliness I feel honors how special you were and are.

Our media seems fascinated with suffering, tragedy, and death. We report the shocking and the unthinkable. But when grief enters our own backyard, we tend to bar the door quickly.

Most of us naturally expect family to love and support us amid difficulty. Some families are super-supportive in tough times, while others are not. Usually, there are a few sympathetic, loving souls in our family circle. We can be grateful for their support and help. And there will be other relatives who simply don't do well in the presence of emotional pain and grief.

We never get over a person, especially a child. That's impossible. When a son or daughter dies, we're crushed. Our hearts are struck. When this massive strand of our life-web is severed, it's often traumatic. Over time, we begin to decipher who is helpful to us in our grief and who is not.

One of our biggest challenges is to spend time with those who are helpful and supportive while limiting our exposure to those who aren't.

We don't get over losing a child. We don't cease to love. We simply get through this time as best we can.

Affirmation: With family, I'll open my heart to those who are supportive, and limit my exposure to those who aren't.

FOR REFLECTION AND/OR JOURNALING

MY GRIEVING HEART:

"Since my child departed, I have felt more vulnerable when..."

I LOSE YOU AGAIN AND AGAIN

FROM THE GRIEVING HEART:

My mind moves so quickly. My heart is a jumble. My emotions are all over the place.

I thought I would be better by now. I don't know what I mean by that exactly.

Maybe I think I should be feeling less, be less upset, be more stable, or be functioning better. It would be nice to be more than a nanosecond away from being a blithering, sobbing idiot.

I don't know what I expected, but this is a longer and harder road than I could have ever imagined.

I miss you. No wonder I feel this way.

I feel scattered and distracted. I can't seem to focus. My concentration is virtually nil. What is happening to me?

I know. It's grief. Losing you is what's happening to me. In some senses, I lose you again and again, day after day.

My life seems like it's in slow motion, yet I sense I need to slow down somehow. I need to slow down my mind and my heart. I can't seem to grasp much of what is happening in my life.

I feel like I can't breathe. My soul needs more oxygen.

I don't know what I expected, but this is harder than I could have ever imagined.

Grief is tough. The loss of a child is excruciating. We naturally wonder how long this painful season will last. Most of us want to feel better as quickly as possible.

Our world is fast paced. We're not used to waiting. We grumble at red lights. We sigh when a web page takes more than a second to load. We expect everything quickly, if not instantly.

Love and relationships operate according to different time schedules. Building the strands of our life web takes time, energy, and work. We attach quickly and deeply to our children. It's a deep, special, unique, and powerful bond. Grieving the loss of a daughter or son can be a long process.

Grief is not a sprint. It's a marathon roller-coaster that endlessly repeats. Over time, we get used to the ups, the downs, and getting thrown around emotionally. Our bruised hearts get bumped again and again. At times, we wince and writhe with the pain. The dull ache of loss seems to permeate our lives.

Grief requires great patience. Accepting ourselves is difficult. Processing all the different facets of our loss is demanding and exhausting. Recovering and adjusting are processes, not destinations.

We must be patient with ourselves. We live in a new world now. The terrain is unfamiliar and the path uncertain. Our child is gone.

The entire world can seem empty. Taking our hearts seriously, moment by moment, is our new priority.

Affirmation: Grieving is a process. I'll be patient with myself and accept myself along the way.

I'M WORRIED ABOUT FORGETTING YOU

FROM THE GRIEVING HEART:

I miss you.

I know I'll never forget you, but I find myself concerned that I'll be less connected to you in the future.

Strange. I fear losing you, even though you are gone.

My mind knows that my sense of closeness to you will most likely diminish as time marches on. It hurts to think about this. You're slowly slipping away from me. I can feel it.

I've known you all your life. How can this be?

I listen to voicemails to remember what your voice sounds like. I look at pictures to remind myself of the features of your face. If it's this way now, what about a year down the road?

Will there be a time when I no longer think of you?

Silly as it sounds, I'm worried about forgetting you. I'm scared you will slowly fade from my mind and heart.

Perhaps I need to talk about you more. Maybe I need to be bold and share memories more than I do. I don't know.

I do know this: I love you.

As time passes, our grief tends to change. For most, the emotions grow less intense and debilitating. The loss settles into our hearts in new ways and often a persistent, dull ache invades us. We might find ourselves thinking about our child less.

Absence only makes the heart grow fonder to a certain extent. Experiencing connection and closeness requires a person's presence, time, and communication. When a child departs, we can slowly lose our sense of them. We're stunned one day to find ourselves wondering what their voice sounded like. We can become frightened of losing them completely. We sense them slipping away from us, bit by bit.

Soon after the loss, we might be obsessed with our child and our memories of them. We're thinking about them constantly. What they did and said. Their voice and their laughter. Our times with them, good and bad. Our heart is focused, and everything is about them.

As we grieve, emotion is released. Our hearts process the loss over time. We slowly begin to adjust. This loss becomes a part of our lives. Our souls begin to grapple with a life without our child's physical presence.

We will never forget them. They permeate our thoughts, personality, words, and actions. They have an always-place in our hearts. But our sense of them will change over time. This is part of healing.

Affirmation: If I feel less connected to you, I won't panic. This is part of grief. You will always be a part of me.

I MUST TALK ABOUT YOU

FROM THE GRIEVING HEART:

You feel more distant now. I know this is natural, but I don't like it.

I don't like any of this. I want you back.

I will not forget you. I won't let that happen. I will talk about you to anyone who will listen. I don't care what they think. I don't care if they think I'm weak or crazy. So what if they look at me and roll their eyes?

I must talk about you. I must find people who will listen.

I will remember and find ways to honor you. I will go on with you, with your influence inside me.

Yet, almost every day I'm saying goodbye to you somehow. Ugh.

You would want me to live and live well. Perhaps living and grieving well is a way I can still love you.

As times goes on, most of us feel more distant from our departed child. This may be disturbing, but it is natural and common. They are no longer in front of us and their absence is becoming part of our new normal.

Many feel they need to say goodbye, slowly and over a period of time, in order to engage in life again. Others resist this, choosing to focus on remembering. Still others refuse to let go in any sense, clinging to any and every thought, memory, or possession that helps keep their child alive in their minds and hearts.

Loss is universal. We all experience it. But grief is deeply personal. Each relationship is unique, and each heart's grief will be unique as well. There is no standard, one-size-fits-all path. We must each find our own way.

Remembering is a part of grieving. Talking about our child and telling their story can be a wonderful way to share ourselves and our hearts with those around us. Finding those we can do this with is important – even essential – to our emotional and physical health.

We will talk about them. We will tell their stories. We will live on, with their influence inside us.

Affirmation: I will talk about you and tell your story – our story. This helps me grieve and is part of loving myself and you.

AM I NEXT?

FROM THE GRIEVING HEART:

I know this sounds morbid, but I find myself wondering, again, who's next?

I don't allow myself to think about this, much less voice it. But deep in a corner of my brain, a fear is lurking. I'm waiting for the next loss. If this could happen to you, then it could happen to anyone, anywhere, at any time.

It could happen to me. Am I next?

I don't like these sad and depressing thoughts. But it's true. Anyone. Anywhere. Any time. Even me, or someone else I love and care about.

I find myself wanting to wrap everyone I see in bubble-wrap and lock everyone I care about away in some impenetrable vault. I want to go where no one leaves and nothing bad can happen to anyone.

Reality is hard. I want things to be good again. I want to feel joy and maybe a little peace. I'm tired of worrying and being afraid.

I miss you.

Fear is common and natural in times of loss. Our world has been upended. Our life-web has been significantly shaken. Our hearts have been jostled. Life has changed. The unknown has reared its ugly head. We wonder about a lot of things.

One loss can lead us to fear another. After a horrific auto accident, it would be natural to not want to drive for a while. Perhaps we get nervous just thinking about getting in a car. We naturally worry about another crash.

In grief, we often come face to face with our own mortality and that of all those we love. If we've had enough loss and tragedy in the past, we can find ourselves waiting for the next disaster to strike. We begin to do life in fortress mode, trying to protect ourselves and those around us from more loss.

Of course, living in fear is not really living. We can learn to acknowledge fear when it comes and release it. We might have to release it again and again. As we grieve, our hearts will process all this, and there will come a day when we're willing to get back in the car again.

As we grieve in healthy ways, we will adjust and heal. We will never be the same. On some level, we might always grieve. We learn to live on while grieving.

Affirmation: When the fear of more loss comes, I'll acknowledge the fear and release it. This is part of grieving and living well.

I THOUGHT I WAS DOING BETTER

FROM THE GRIEVING HEART:

I thought I was doing better.

Then I saw an ad that reminded me of you.
It struck my heart like lightning.

For a moment, I was stunned...paralyzed. Then
the flood of sadness poured out of me.

I felt as if I had lost you all over again.

Is this ever going to end? Why can't I control myself?

Am I making progress, or going backward? Am I stuck?

I know I've said this kind of thing before –
probably a dozen times, if not more.

I don't think I'm stuck. I just feel lost at times. I feel a
little stronger...and then discover I'm still a mess.

I guess that's the grief roller-coaster. I think things have leveled out,
and then I suddenly find myself being whipped around again.

Patience. Yes. Grief requires patience. I must be patient
with myself. I'm worth that. You would want that.

Breathe. Again. One breath at a time. One moment at a time.

Grieving the loss of a child is such a back-and-forth, up-and-down emotional process that we can get turned around. We wonder which end is up. What does progress look like? Will there ever be a stable routine again?

After a while, our emotions might level out. Life gets a tad bit smoother. Then we get hit with another grief burst. Another anvil whacks us out of a clear blue sky. We're shocked and stunned all over again. The grief feels so familiar that we can end up believing we're back where we started.

Nothing could be further from the truth.

Grief bursts will come. Triggers are everywhere. Our heart wounds can be poked by anything, anytime, anywhere. As we've said before, we can't protect ourselves from these sudden intrusions, but we can decide beforehand how we will handle them. We can let the grief come. It's natural and healthy. We can feel the emotions, as we are able.

Some talk out loud about what's happening inside them. Others process these bursts through writing. Still others share with safe people they trust.

Again, these grief bursts are common and normal. They will come. They will go. Our hearts are remembering. Our emotions are declaring our love. We miss our child.

Being kind to ourselves by being patient with ourselves is vital.

Affirmation: When grief bursts come, I will breathe deeply and feel them through. These times are steps forward, not backward.

FOR REFLECTION AND/OR JOURNALING

MY GRIEVING HEART:

"When I think about other people's children, I find myself…"

I WANT TO HONOR YOU

FROM THE GRIEVING HEART:

We had so many wonderful times together. I have so many memories tied to special days on the calendar.

One of those special days is coming up. I can feel the dread as it approaches.

I want to remember you and grieve well on that day. I want to honor you.

I've decided to write you a letter telling you how I'm doing and what I miss about you, about me, and about us. I know it will be emotional, but I believe it will be good. I feel a little shy... but determined.

You're not here, but I still love you. I will express that love, as I can, when I can.

Maybe as time goes on, I will dread these special days less. Perhaps I can use them well and eventually they will bring joy instead of sadness. I choose to believe so.

I guess I could write a letter to you any day, couldn't I? I don't know why I didn't think of that before.

I'm thinking of you and smiling. That feels good.

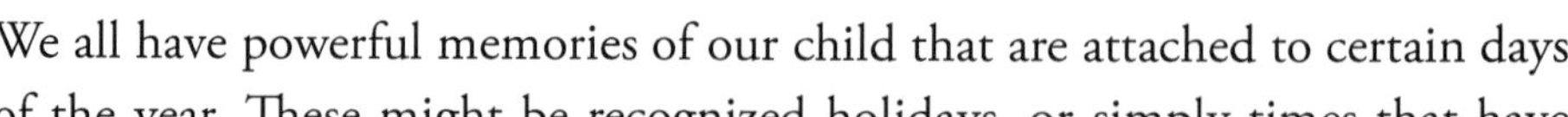

We all have powerful memories of our child that are attached to certain days of the year. These might be recognized holidays, or simply times that have significance for us and our relationship with our daughter or son. In any case, it's good to be aware of these days and prepare for them.

Many choose to do something meaningful to honor their child on these days. Writing letters can be effective as this focuses our attention and slows down our distracted minds and hearts. We can express ourselves specifically and intentionally. Even if no one else reads it, our hearts have expressed themselves in a proactive and healthy way.

Making a simple plan for special days can help us prepare and relieve a lot of potential angst. It's helpful to be able to express what's inside us somehow. Writing, drawing, painting, sculpting, and talking out loud are possibilities. Giving a donation in their name, serving somewhere in their honor, or continuing a tradition they enjoyed are also good options.

As we grieve, we can find ways to make these days not only more bearable but good. Tears will be shed, but there will be smiles too.

Affirmation: Rather than dreading special days,
I will make plans to remember and honor you.
This is part of loving myself and you.

I NEED TO BE REAL

FROM THE GRIEVING HEART:

Writing that letter was good for me. I cried, smiled, and laughed. I'm glad I did it.

In fact, I'm going to start writing more often. I guess people call that a journal. I don't want a diary. I'm not interested in simply recording where I went and what I did. I want to express my heart. I'm eager to process this grief.

I'll begin by simply talking about what's happening inside me – what I'm thinking and feeling. I'm guessing there's no right or wrong way to do this. Giving my heart a safe place to vent is what's most important to me.

I have some safe people I can talk to, but even then, I hold back a little. I don't want to be too shocking. When I write, I feel freer to be me.

As I express my heart, I'm struck again by the depth of my love for you. Grieving your loss is more like running a cross country race rather than a 100-yard dash.

Even though I can't see the finish line, I'm beginning to run the race with more confidence.

I want to make you proud. I will win this race for "us".

When I write, I can be real. I need to be real.

Many have found keeping a journal to be a key to their recovery and adjustment after the loss of a child. We can express thoughts and emotions honestly and openly. There are things we might never be able to say in front of another person, but we can get them down on paper.

In grief, getting things out is important. Expressing what's inside is crucial. Writing can help us do this.

Some can easily record what's happening inside, while others need more direction. Many find writing prompts to be helpful. Here are some examples:

- What I miss most today is…
- I find myself most concerned about…
- One of my fondest memories of you is…
- Things that have surprised me about grief are…
- If I could go back, I would…
- Some of the things I learned from you are…
- When I think about the future, I wonder…

There is no end to the possible prompts that could be used. Our hearts heal as they express themselves, bit by bit, over time. A journal is one more way we can "talk" about our child, tell their story, and honor them.

Affirmation: My heart needs to continually express itself to be healthy and to heal. I'll find a way to do this.

EVERYONE MATTERS

FROM THE GRIEVING HEART:

My heart is changing.

Things that used to be important aren't anymore. Nothing matters except people.

As I look back, my biggest regrets involve relationships. Something I said. Something I did. Things I wish I could do over.

I have hurt others, and others have hurt me. My heart has wounds. Every heart does.

You weren't perfect. I'm certainly not perfect either. We hurt each other along the way. I have regrets back there. Perhaps you do too.

There are no do-overs. But there is forgiveness. I forgive you. Please forgive me.

Even though you're gone, I want nothing between us except love. I want my heart to be as clear and clean as possible.

I don't talk about these wounds much. I just live with them and hope that somehow everything will work out okay. My problem is that my wounds keep getting bumped by life. And then they hurt. Pain always gets my attention.

You mattered. That's why losing you is painful. I matter, though at times it doesn't feel that way. Everyone matters. We all long to be loved, don't we?

Your departure has taught me so much. Now is the time to live.

Love now. Express kindness now. Say what
I need and want to say now.

There may not be another opportunity.

People matter. Each one. I will remember that today.

I continue to learn from you, my child.

Life is about people. We come out of the womb looking for connection and love. Our child was dependent on us for everything. We embraced them, held them, and showered them with love.

Our relationships with our children become some of the thickest in our web. We were all children at one time. Deep down, we're still children at heart. Everywhere we go, we naturally search for safety and unconditional acceptance. We want to love and be loved. We grow and thrive when we feel seen, heard, and significant.

Most people find love by giving it. We find safety the same way. Safe, loving people tend to attract others who also value safety and close connections.

Along the way, we get hurt, and we hurt others. Our hearts are wounded. This affects the way we approach life and relationships. When a child dies, our sense of safety can take a hit. We've loved, and now we've lost. This can be excruciatingly painful.

If we're willing, the loss of a son or daughter can teach us to live more meaningful and significant lives. Relationships take on new importance. We now know that all we have is the present moment. Nothing else is guaranteed. We set our sights on expressing our hearts, saying what we need to say and doing what we need to do.

In the end, our wounded hearts still need the same things: love and safety. We can give some of that away today. As we do, our love for others can become a salve to our own wounded hearts.

Affirmation: I will live and love today, one
person, one moment at a time.

I DIDN'T KNOW WHAT I DIDN'T KNOW

FROM THE GRIEVING HEART:

They say confession is good for the soul. I've been writing in my journal about this. Losing you has caused me to consider my own life more deeply.

Through my grief, I can look back and see mistake after mistake. Errors galore. Mainly, I see how I've judged others who were in pain. I have many regrets.

Then again, I didn't know what I didn't know. I had not experienced loss like this, so how could I understand significant emotional pain? We don't know until we've been there.

I spoke of things I didn't know anything about. I distanced myself from people who were hurting. I disappeared from some lives. I did to others the things I've been angry at others for doing to me.

Life has interesting twists. Perhaps I should contact some of these people and apologize. That might do us both good. I don't know. It's a bit scary to contemplate being that vulnerable.

For now, I will go on using my journal to express my deepest pain and the mistakes that I've made along the way. It feels good, like my soul is being cleansed.

You're still teaching me, even through your departure. Thank you. I miss you.

In many cases, loss causes us to look back at our own behavior and wince. Because we had not known significant grief, many of us were less than sensitive to those in pain around us. We were uncomfortable. We didn't know what to say. As time went on, perhaps we grew impatient with them. Maybe we withdrew and distanced ourselves.

We see life differently now. We know the pain of loss and the frustration of being misunderstood. We have experienced the hurt of evaluation, judgment, and rejection at a time when our hearts were broken and bleeding. Guilt can raise its head.

Personal recognition and confession can be profoundly good and healing. As our hearts own up to what we thought, said, and did, we can better release the past and live fuller, more meaningful lives now. Confession allows us to look back, evaluate, and bring some closure to painful situations. There may even be scenarios where we can apologize or make amends.

Our hearts do better when we own up to the truth, as painful as that might be. As we do, we'll be able to engage with life and others more fully. We'll become more authentic. We'll give away more love and safety, and experience more of them in return.

The loss of a child has many lessons for us. They're still teaching us, even though they're no longer with us.

Why not learn as much as we can?

Affirmation: Losing you has taught me I can look back, own the hurt I've caused, and live more meaningfully than ever before.

I CONTINUE TO LEARN FROM YOU

FROM THE GRIEVING HEART:

Yesterday was important. I received an email from a good friend. All they said was, "I'm thinking about you."

I was amazed how that phrase affected me. I was comforted and felt loved.

So simple. "I'm thinking about you."

Words are both crucial and overrated. It seems like where there are many words, there is misunderstanding and hurt. I can be wordy, but I'm learning that the value is not in the words, but in thinking about and seeing the other person.

Losing you has taught me this. Words fix nothing. Platitudes are empty. Hearts matter. Presence counts.

"I'm thinking of you."

Nice. I need to be thought of.

I think I'll write to another grieving heart today. My message will be simple.

"I'm thinking of you."

I continue to learn from you. The ripple effects of being your parent continue. Thank you.

In grief and in life, what we say and what is said to us has great power. Words can hurt or heal. In general, however, when grief emotions are intense, the fewer the words, the better.

More important than what's said is the heart behind the words. Is the other person being thought of? Are the words more about the speaker or the recipient? Not knowing what another grieving heart might be thinking or feeling at any given moment, "I'm thinking of you," can be a wonderfully expressive statement.

It's nice to be thought of. We're being remembered with concern and affection, without evaluation, judgment, or attempts to change or fix. When grieving hearts are met where they are, even for a moment, good occurs.

Even with shattered hearts, we can do good. When we connect with other grieving souls out of genuine concern for their welfare, our own needs are partially met. We receive by giving.

We can think of each other often. We can express our affection and concern simply and authentically. The results for all of us could be extraordinary over time.

Affirmation: I can express simple kindness to other grieving hearts. This helps all of us.

FOR RELFLECTION AND/OR JOURNALING

MY GRIEVING HEART:

"If someone were to ask me how to grieve well, I would say…"

I WILL USE MY GRIEF FOR GOOD

FROM THE GRIEVING HEART:

I talked to another grieving heart yesterday. They said something that struck me.

"What did I ever do to deserve this?" they asked.

I blinked.

"Maybe this is my just reward for all my miscues and mistakes," they continued.

I also heard the opposite: "My loved one didn't deserve this. I don't think I deserve this either. Why is life so unfair?"

I don't know which it is. Perhaps neither. How can we as humans make judgments about such things? We don't know. We can't know.

It happened. You're gone. This is reality now. I must find ways to live on. I want to live well, remembering and honoring you along the way.

I will let go of blame. It serves no purpose. I will invest in my heart. I will never be the same, and I don't want to be. But I will heal and grow through this.

And I will use my grief for good. I will honor you.

When it comes to what happens and why, there is much we don't understand. We control little, yet we have profound influence over what and who we're connected to. The ripple effects of our lives are widespread and extraordinary.

We don't know everything — not even close. We can't be in two places at once. We have influence, but we are far less powerful than we think when we're talking about keeping bad things from happening to our children or other people we care about.

Our hearts might continue to question, but through the grief process, we often come to the point of accepting some of what we can't comprehend. In our own way, we must make some sense of what happened, and then do the best we can to live on in light of it.

When we release the need to understand everything, we open our hearts up to accept this new reality. We start adjusting to our current situation. Our new normal begins to take shape.

We learn to take our souls and bodies seriously. We discover that loving ourselves is one of the greatest gifts we can give ourselves and our departed son or daughter. We begin to jettison whatever keeps us from healing and growing.

We will never be the same, but we can still live with great significance and impact.

Affirmation: Part of grieving is learning to let go of what is no longer helpful. I want to travel light and make a difference.

PERHAPS LETTING GO ISN'T WHAT I THOUGHT

FROM THE GRIEVING HEART:

I hear a lot about letting go. At first, this irked me. Let go? How do I do that? I don't want to!

But perhaps letting go isn't what I thought.

On this grief journey, I've discovered that I must let go of certain things.

If I want to live, I must let the past be what it was. I also must grieve the future I anticipated but now will never be. I must learn to live well here without your physical presence.

I'm working to let go of guilt, shame, and blame. I want to release the wounds and mistakes of the past and be burdened by them no longer. I want to remember and honor you while engaging in life and doing the most good I can.

Above all, I want to release my expectations. Most of the time, they simply set me up for disappointment. I will plan yet hold those plans loosely. All I can do is become the best version of me possible. I choose to focus on that and take what comes.

Letting go doesn't mean forgetting you. It means embracing and loving you in new ways.

I will practice letting go – one thing, one moment at a time.

When a grieving heart hears the phrase "letting go," our first inclination is resistance. We assume that letting go means giving up our memories or leaving our child behind. Since we're wired for connection, our instinct is to cling to them with all our might.

But what if letting go could mean something different? What if it means releasing the things that weigh us down in the grief process — things like critical influences, toxic people, unhelpful thought patterns, or self-numbing addictions? What if letting go refers to intentionally releasing what's not healthy to more fully embrace what is?

Many discover that letting go and grieving well are synonymous. As we take our hearts seriously and express our grief in healthy ways, our departed children assume new roles in our lives. As we adjust to their absence, we begin to appreciate things about them we might have missed before. As we accept our loss, we might also be embracing them in new ways.

Grief is a truly mysterious process. It is not a program or checklist, but rather a meandering path that often doubles back on itself. Its dizzying twists and turns can be confusing, but as we continue our journey, we discover we're heading somewhere.

We don't need to know it all. We can't. But at any given moment, we can choose to release what burdens us and lean forward into what's coming.

Affirmation: Letting go may not be what I thought. I can release what was and embrace what is, one moment at a time.

MY GRIEF IS CHANGING

FROM THE GRIEVING HEART:

My grief is changing. I can feel it.

I miss you. I always will. But the missing is somehow less intense. My heart must be adjusting to you not being here.

Ugh. I feel guilty saying that.

I must remind myself that we're talking about your physical presence. Your influence – your thoughts, words, and actions – will always be here, inside me. You continue to live and express yourself to me and through me in many ways.

Life is so different now. I'm different. I used to try to control everything. Losing you has taught me just how little I can control.

Life is not what I expected. Things have not gone how I planned. I've had my share of surprises, and not all of them have been good. Pain and grief are good teachers, if I'm willing to learn from them.

I want to travel lighter. I want to live more in freedom than in fear. I want to live well without having to feel in control. This life is short, and I want to make a difference.

In some ways, you have taught me this. You continue to influence my life greatly, though you are no longer here. You are a gift to me. You always have been.

Thank you.

Not many of us live free. Many go through the motions, not thinking much about life or the future. Some live unevaluated lives focused on avoiding pain and being comfortable. Many are on a treadmill they can't seem to step off.

Burdened by expectations, worries, and fears, we slog through our days. We work, strive, plot, and plan. Then death or disaster comes, and our illusions of control are dealt a shattering blow. We grieve not only the loss of our child, but also the death of our world as we knew it. We mourn our loss of perceived control.

As we've said before, we don't control much — perhaps only the thoughts we allow to dwell in our minds and the resulting words and actions. We have influence but not control over circumstances, other people, and life in general. In the end, we're better off accepting this reality, abandoning our futile attempts at control, and focusing on becoming the best people we can be.

Loss and grief can instruct us. We can choose to travel lighter now. We can live with greater purpose and meaning. We can practice living more in the present moment, rather than dwelling in the past or the future.

This is all a process, and most of us are slow learners. We breathe deeply. We lean forward. We try to be patient with ourselves along the way.

Affirmation: I'll keep breathing deeply, try to control less, and practice living in the present moment.

WHY DO WE BURY OUR GRIEF AND PAIN?

FROM THE GRIEVING HEART:

As I drove around yesterday, I found myself looking at the people in the vehicles around me. "How many of them are grieving?" I wondered.

Probably many more than I realize.

I believe that most people are hurting, worried, or fearful. After all, everyone has been wounded, and all of us have experienced loss of some kind. We just fake it. We put on a good face. We wear masks.

I pulled into a parking lot and sat there thinking. The collective pain out there stunned me.

Why doesn't anyone talk about this? Why do we bury our grief and pain?

No wonder the world seems on the verge of exploding from time to time.

Inside, I felt my loss somehow take its place among all the other losses of the world. Maybe I felt a little of others' pain.

I know I've said it before, but I'll write it again. I'll put my grief to work. I am small, but I matter. I want to honor you. I want to make a difference.

When loss strikes, most of us naturally pull inward. We're shaken and vulnerable. We're stunned and need to catch our breath. Then we begin to feel the pain and sadness. If the loss is great enough, it can begin to take over our entire existence.

When a person is in great pain, it's hard to think about anything else. Life becomes about endurance and managing the pain as well as possible. Although this might be the stage we're in, this phase is not forever. Pain and suffering are not our new life. This is a season of loss and grief.

As we process the loss of our daughter or son, our hearts begin to adjust and our grief changes. We still love and miss them, but the pain is different. We begin to learn to live on, with a hole in our hearts.

Our experience with loss can sensitize us to the grief and pain of those around us. Loss is everywhere. Hearts have been broken and dreams crushed. Plans have been shattered and souls shaken. We can put our grief to work and meet hurting hearts where they are. We can help bring comfort, perspective, and hope.

We're in this together. We desperately need each other. We can all make more of an impact than we realize.

Affirmation: Losing you has sensitized me to the pain of others. Even while hurting, I can comfort others.

I'M SWIMMING UPSTREAM

FROM THE GRIEVING HEART:

I've come to a conclusion. I can either let the world and circumstances set the agenda for my life, or I can be about something bigger and better.

When I lost you, I longed for listening ears and compassionate hearts to be with me in this. Instead, what I got most of the time was impatience, judgment, and criticism. People's reactions only added to my pain rather than helping relieve it.

This isn't right. And I believe it can change. At least, I can choose to not be one of the mass of judgmental voices out there.

I choose to have a compassionate heart.

I will stop and see the pain of others.

I will take a moment, look in their eyes, and enter their world. I want to be a safe person that feels a tiny portion of their grief and reminds them that they are not alone.

I sense that I'm swimming upstream, but I'll bet there are others like me out there. There must be other grieving hearts who have decided to be a part of the solution to the world's pain and grief.

I will put my grief experience to work. I will pay attention and look for opportunities.

As we move through our grief, we begin to be more aware of the struggles of others. There are wounds everywhere. Many have departed and died. Almost every heart has at least one hole in it. We're all missing someone.

Grief can produce in us new reservoirs of love and compassion. There is power and healing in reaching out to another hurting soul. We can be the soft hearts and listening ears that we ourselves longed for in our grief journey.

We have been there. We know. We understand that grieving hearts don't need fixing, judgment, or criticism. They need someone safe, someone they can call on when needed to simply be with them. We have learned that showing up and being available is a powerful offer of support and kindness.

Our hearts have been broken. Our life web has been shaken. One of our thickest strands has been severed. Our lives have been upended. Our child is gone. Even while in pain, we can extend a hand to other grieving hearts. When two souls that know grief find each other, healing occurs.

We know the problems surrounding grief in our world. We can be a part of the solution.

Affirmation: Now that I know grief, I can be part of the solution for other grieving hearts. I will show up, listen, and love.

FOR REFLECTION AND/OR JOURNALING

MY GRIEVING HEART:

"As I look back, I can see my grief changing over time. For example…"

TRIGGERS ARE EVERYWHERE

FROM THE GRIEVING HEART:

Yesterday was tough. Everywhere I went, there seemed to be reminders of you. Triggers were everywhere. Grief bursts riddled the day.

I wondered what was happening. I thought perhaps I was losing it, again. I tried to collect myself, slow down, and breathe deeply. After all this time, I'm still surprised how difficult simply breathing is when grief emotions strike.

Then that old fear hit me. "What if all this grief work didn't help? What if the grief returns and takes over my life again? What if healing is an illusion and I'm never be able to climb out of this pit?"

I kept trying to breathe deeply and began talking to myself.

"Be kind to yourself. Be patient with yourself. This is grief. Just grieve."

In the middle of it all, I reached out to one of my safe people. Their voice was so calming. I could almost see their smile over the phone. It was like they expected me to have another day like this at some point.

"Just breathe and grieve. This is natural and normal," they said.

Breathe and grieve.

Many naturally think that once their grief journey gets to a certain point that there will be no more bad days or emotional pain. Heart bruises can be bumped at any time, and the pain can be intense.

There is no time limit on grief bursts. We have all experienced more loss than we realize, and the grief can build up slowly over time. Suddenly it needs to be released. Grief will be expressed. This is natural, normal, and healthy.

The question is not if we will have more grief bursts, but when. When they come, we breathe through them. We can be patient with ourselves and remind our hearts that this grief is okay. Instead of fighting it, we can simply grieve.

If we're questioning our progress or our sanity, then reaching out to a safe person is an excellent option. Those who know grief can give us perspective and be extremely reassuring. Grieving hearts often need reassurance.

When these grief attacks happen to others, we can be the reassuring voice. "Just breathe and grieve. This is natural and normal."

Affirmation: I will be patient with myself and remember that grief bursts can happen at any time, even months or years down the road.

IT WILL BE HARD, BUT IT CAN STILL BE GOOD

FROM THE GRIEVING HEART:

Today is an important day. It's the anniversary of your death. I've missed you. I miss you still.

I dreaded this day, but at least I planned for it. I was tempted to stick my head in the sand and wait it out, but I knew that wouldn't be honoring to you or loving toward myself.

I will remember you today. I will light a candle in your honor. I will write you a letter. I will breathe deeply through all of this. I will be kind to myself, patient with myself, and grieve.

I will open my heart to others and allow them to express concern for me today. I will receive gladly any gestures of kindness from friends or loved ones that may come my way.

Several of my safe people know what today is. I will reach out to them at some point. It's good to have someone in this with me.

I will get out among people today and remind myself that I still live in a world of people and relationships. I will focus on seeing those around me, knowing that they too have known loss in some way.

I will make today count. It will be hard, but it can still be good.

I still miss you. I always will.

Death anniversaries are difficult. These days can be hard for many years, perhaps even the rest of our lives. Along with the pain these times naturally bring, we can also use these days to help us grieve and to honor our child.

We can make a simple plan to remember them. We can do something they would enjoy. We can honor them by giving to or serving a cause that reminds us of them. We can write a letter, set up an empty chair, go to a favorite place, or engage in a special activity.

We loved them and love them still. We know them. What seems to fit best? What would help us grieve and also honor them? Can we involve others somehow?

We know this day will be hard, but it can still be good. It can be meaningful and healing. If we focus on expressing love, we can't go wrong no matter how we choose to honor them.

This anniversary is important. Every year it will stand out. We can plan for it, and make it count.

Affirmation: I will make the anniversary of your death count. It will be hard, but it can still be good.

ONE DAY AT A TIME

FROM THE GRIEVING HEART:

I'm looking back today. I see a lot of pain. I also see many blessings.

I remember how others treated me. Some said they would be there, then disappeared. Others avoided me and even pretended not to see me in public. Still others said unhelpful, even hurtful things.

The world didn't seem to care or even be fazed by your loss. It scurried on as if nothing happened. I was angry, frustrated, sad, and depressed. I felt guilty, stunned, and confused. I thought I was going crazy.

I discovered who was safe and who wasn't. A few came close and entered my pain. They listened. They cared. Their presence made all the difference.

I longed for your presence. Your absence permeated everything. My world changed. I changed.

I grieved. I learned. I grew. It still hurts, but I'm trying to use the pain for good.

The journey continues, one day at a time. I will live with meaning and make a difference in this hurting world. I want to positively impact the lives of those who are grieving.

I'll use this giant hole in my heart to help bring hope and healing to others.

Grief alters our world. It changes everything because it changes us. No one is the same after a loss. No one.

Grief also reveals us. It unveils our hearts and shows what matters to us most deeply. Loss turns us inside out.

The loss of a child and the resulting grief can teach us much. We discover what's most important in life. We learn what's trivial and mere fluff. Loss can shake us into new and more positive ways of thinking, speaking, and living. None of us wants loss or pain, but once they come, there is much we can receive if we're willing.

We also begin to discern things about others that we didn't know before. We learn to recognize who's helpful and who's not. We see better what relationships are safe for us and which ones might be toxic. Clearer vision can enable wiser decision-making.

Grief is hard and painful, but it can bring many blessings. We will always miss our child, but now we can make their lives and memory count in new ways.

Affirmation: Loss has taught me what's important and how to live with more purpose and impact. I'm grateful for this.

I WANT TO LIVE TODAY AS BEST I CAN

FROM THE GRIEVING HEART:

You matter. I matter. The people around me matter. I will use my grief to love and serve.

I'll hurt from time to time. I have a dull ache deep inside that may never go away. I'm okay with that. It reminds me of you. The thought of you brings more smiles than tears these days, for which I'm thankful.

I could walk around afraid of death, separation, or what's going to happen next. Or I could choose to live courageously and make each day count. Personally, the latter seems easier and a lot more fulfilling.

I will live with purpose. Your death stunned me and broke my heart. Somehow, the shattered pieces have come together again and are ready to live. The color is coming back into my world. My heart will never be the same, but I believe it can be even better, because of you.

I will live today, as best I can. I will see others and attempt to take a glimpse into their hearts. I want to be more understanding of their needs and their pain. I will act with kindness and compassion. I will love, as much as I can, in each situation.

One day, one person, one interaction, one moment at a time.

Life is full of loss. We experience it more than we realize, in more forms than we can imagine. Most settle into a pattern of coping as best they can with the hits that come. Some choose to attempt to dull the pain with various addictions. Others decide to take their hearts seriously, learn to grieve well, and heal.

Why do we grieve? Because we love. We connect, relate, grow close, trust, and love. When loss severs a strand of our life web, the pain we experience is natural. Our grief proclaims our love.

Since we're meant for connection, saying goodbye is hard. In the case of a child, farewells are excruciating. This takes time. Most parents end up saying farewell in bits and pieces. Our hearts process the loss, trying to understand and find some solid ground in a suddenly shifting world.

If we embrace grief's lessons, we can end up appreciating people even more. We can live more in the present, seeing and hearing those around us. We can be intentionally kind and deeply compassionate. We can live with quiet power and purpose.

Most people feel more significant and fulfilled when they're expressing love and serving others. Perhaps doing so gets us more in touch with who we really are – unique, special individuals doing life with and for one another.

We love, and we grieve, one day, one person, one moment at a time.

Affirmation: I will make your loss count. I will love and live life one interaction, one moment at a time.

FOR REFLECTION AND/OR JOURNALING

MY GRIEVING HEART:

"When I think of using my grief for good and to serve others, I think of…."

CONCLUDING THOUGHTS: A PERSONAL PERSPECTIVE ON LOSS, GRIEF, AND EMOTIONAL PAIN

"Mourn with those who mourn."

– The Apostle Paul

"In this world, you will have trouble."

– Jesus Christ

Thank you for taking your heart seriously and reading this book. I hope you found it comforting and helpful. Most of all, I trust you know you're not alone. Grief is a lonely road, but we can travel it together.

I would like to conclude by sharing my personal perspective on loss, grief, and emotional pain in the hope that somehow my experience might be beneficial to you in your journey.

I AM A FELLOW STRUGGLER

As I mentioned in the introductory chapter, I am a fellow struggler. I battle daily with issues stemming from the losses I've endured and continue to face. I stumble a lot in life.

I am a follower of Jesus Christ. I'm also inconsistent and far from perfect. I get confused, frustrated, and anxious at times. But Jesus is my life, and this influences my thoughts, actions, and how I write.

Whether you come from a different faith orientation or perhaps claim no faith at all, my goal is not to convince you of anything or cause distress of any kind. My purpose is to encourage you by sharing what has been helpful to me in navigating this up-and-down existence of grief and loss.

So please take the following for what it is: my story. Your story is your own.

MY EARLY STORY

I lost both grandfathers so early I don't remember them. Due to dementia, one grandmother never knew who I was. Though I had relatives nearby, my nuclear family was isolated and relationally distant from them. As a child, I remember feeling sad and lonely most of the time.

I lost chunks of my early childhood to repetitive, traumatic sexual abuse. This shaped my view of myself, others, the world, and God. My sadness and loneliness grew. My family experienced other close losses, and I remember the atmosphere of grief that blanketed our home. It was stifling and had a tinge of hopelessness to it.

In junior high school, a good friend died suddenly over the Christmas holidays. He sat right in front of me in homeroom. He was so bright, fun, full of promise, and healthy. I remember thinking, "How can such things happen?"

My home environment was volatile. My parents separated and divorced in my early teens. By default, I stayed with Mom. She had serious mental health issues and slipped deeper into a world of grandiose delusions. It wasn't a good situation. I moved in with Dad.

The next six months were some of the best of my life. Dad was stable, and his presence provided a strong sense of safety. Then one Sunday afternoon, he collapsed in front of me of a massive heart attack. I picked up the phone and stared at it. I couldn't even remember 911.

I've had many flashbacks about that day. I've replayed it in my mind hundreds of times. I found ways to blame myself. I felt so incredibly powerless.

Though they were able to resuscitate his heart, Dad never regained consciousness. I sat by his hospital bed, held his hand, and said everything I could possibly think of to say. I remember gazing at his face for long periods of time, as if I was trying to memorize it.

I knew in my heart he was already gone. I knew it when I found him on the kitchen floor of our apartment.

After a week in the hospital, my brother and I gave permission to turn off life support. Dad died a few hours later.

My world, as I knew it, was over.

I was 15.

I moved back in with Mom, who was even more unstable than before. After attempting to take her own life, she went into psychiatric care. In many ways, I had lost my mom too.

Functionally, I was now an orphan. I wondered where the next hit was going to come from.

In my simple teenage way, I accepted reality. Life was difficult. Bad stuff was going to happen. In this world, I was going to have trouble.

At the same time, all of this was more than I could handle. My anxiety, anger, and depression began to leak out. I began engaging in risky behavior. Some of my friends wondered if I had a death wish of some kind.

Soon after this, I was taken in by my best friend's family. As I walked into their home, I felt a profound sense of safety.

Even though they already had four kids, they loved, accepted, and supported me in every way imaginable. Some days I wondered if this could be real. It was so good, in fact, that I simply couldn't take it all in.

One day, I asked the dad why he would take in a kid like me and make me a part of his family. He smiled and said, "Gary, with what Jesus Christ did for us, how could we not do this for you?"

Jesus was not new to me. I began going to church when I was 10. I was hurting and looking for hope. I got to know Jesus there. I wasn't interested in religion. I needed love and relationship.

Now, here he was again, this Jesus.

AN ADVENTURE OF HEALING

I went to college and studied Psychology. I immersed myself in service and found myself surrounded by troubled, wounded people. People like me. Ever since, my adult life has been focused on helping hurting people heal and grow. As I give, I heal a little bit more.

Looking back, I can see many mother and father figures that emerged along the way. These people accepted, loved, and mentored me in significant ways. Though my own parents were gone, God continued to provide the wisdom, insight, and guidance I needed through others.

"A father to the fatherless, a defender of widows,
is God in his holy dwelling. God sets the lonely in families..."
(Psalm 68:5-6a).

I experienced the truth of these words many times. Everywhere I went, God created a sense of family for me. I have been blessed indeed.

As I got older, the losses continued to pile up, as they do with all of us. I lost more relatives, friends, and co-workers. With each loss, the pain of past losses came visiting, adding to the grief of the present. As a missionary and pastor, I was frequently around emotional pain, grief, and loss.

Then my marriage of almost three decades ended in a divorce I did not want or agree with. The pain and confusion were intense. For the next several years, I questioned almost everything. The seemingly sudden death of my marriage was devastating. I felt my heart go numb, and then harden.

Normally positive and eager to trust others, my heart turned cautious. I walled myself off emotionally. I lived in fortress mode.

As I look back on my life, I can see several patterns. The biggest pattern is that when I seek God, wait, and don't try to make something happen, God surprises me. That's exactly what he did, again.

Through a truly miraculous set of coincidences, my heart warmed to an amazing lady who had lost her husband to pancreatic cancer. I didn't expect my soulmate to simply walk into my life one day. I knew God still has a plan for me, but he has completely surprised me with how good and delightful he can be.

Looking back, God has taken the pain and rubble of my losses and sculpted them into something that...well, I don't even have words to describe it.

When people hear I work as a hospice chaplain and grief counselor, most inevitably say, "I don't know how you do what you do." Yes, it's hard. It's heavy. I'm in the presence of death every day. Grief is part of the air I breathe. And I wouldn't trade it for anything. I get to enter people's lives at a sensitive and vulnerable time. I have the honor of walking with others through some of their darkest valleys.

Who else gets to do that?

WE'RE ALL DIFFERENT, BUT WE HAVE MUCH IN COMMON.

So many are hurting. Different people with diverse backgrounds, unique relationships, deeply personal losses, and different faiths. But we all have this in common: we are human, and we experience loss.

I believe God not only knows our pain but feels it with us. We're designed for relationship. Separation is hard. Hearts break and shatter. God knows this. He walks with us, though many times we are unaware of his presence.

Then there is this Jesus character. The Bible declares him to be God who has taken on human flesh. He came among us, walked with us, and experienced the joy, delight, and love that quality relationships can bring. He also tasted the ugliness of injustice, deception, manipulation, rejection, betrayal, abuse, torture, and violent death. No one truly understood him. He knows loneliness. He is well acquainted with grief.

If he is God in human flesh, believing that he rose from the dead isn't a stretch for me. Rather, it seems plausible and natural. I believe he conquered death to offer me something better than the disappointment, pain, frustration, and loss of this world. I think he still conquers death, every day, in my life and in the lives of others.

Jesus knows. He knows grief, and he knows me. He shares my loneliness. This companion has made all the difference for me. He shows up in interesting ways. He brings the right people at the right time. His presence is constant. He reminds me this life is not all there is. Death has been conquered.

Again, this is my story. My prayer is that it brings some comfort and hope to you amid your loss and pain. We will never be the same, but we can still live with great purpose. Healing is possible.

THE HEALING ADVENTURE CONTINUES

I close with something Jesus himself said that has been profoundly comforting to me. I hope you find it so too.

"I have said these things to you so that in me you might have peace. In this world, you will have trouble. Take heart. I have overcome the world. So do not let your hearts be troubled, and do not be afraid."

– (John 16:33)

In this world, we will face trouble. Loss is part of our daily existence. Much of life is about overcoming.

Breathe deeply. Take your heart seriously. You matter.

AN INVITATION TO MAKE A DIFFERENCE

When we serve others who are hurting, our own hearts heal a little. Over time, the comfort and caring we share with those around us can add up, bringing relief and greater health to our own wounded souls.

In the latter portion of this book, we began thinking about how to use our grief to make a difference in this world and in the lives of others. If this interests you, I would like to invite you to consider becoming a part of my Difference Maker Community. As a group, we are focused on making a positive, healing impact in the lives of those around us – especially other grieving hearts.

For more information, please contact me at contact@garyroe.com. Simply say, "I would like to know more about the Difference Maker Community," and I will respond to you personally.

Together, I believe we can make a massive difference.

Warmly, Gary

Help us reach more grieving hearts
who have lost a child.
Share this link:
https://www.garyroe.com/comfort-series/
Together, we can make a difference.

SUMMARY OF GRIEF AFFIRMATIONS

I'm stunned. Dazed. I must breathe…

Because my love is deep, my grief may be intense. Tears are natural and healthy.

I give myself permission to be sad. I will let the grief come.

It's okay if I get angry. I will find healthy ways to express my anger.

Loss is confusing. I'll be patient with myself.

Money and financial matters can be frustrating and draining. I'll handle them one at a time.

Life is surreal. I'm trying to make sense of things. This will take time.

There are many things I won't understand. I'll be patient with myself.

I'm missing you. Feeling alone is natural when grieving.

My heart is my most important possession. I'll take care of it today. I'll handle what I can, as I can.

I may feel numb at times. That's okay. My heart is working to manage the unmanageable.

I'll work on accepting myself while grieving, one moment, one step at a time.

All my relationships seem to be changing. I don't like this. I will hold all things loosely, forgive quickly, and grieve as best as I know how.

I feel crazy sometimes because losing you is insane. I will learn to accept that I'm not at my mental best right now.

My life is disturbed, so it makes sense my sleep would be too. I'll focus on grieving well and trust this will change over time.

I'll ride this grief roller coaster as best I can, one moment at a time.

Though some people might disappoint me, I will grieve as best I can, given the circumstances.

Parenting feels impossible right now. I'll focus on taking care of myself and grieving in healthy ways. I'll face life one thing, one moment at a time.

When fear comes, I'll try to acknowledge it, identify it, and release it.

When anxiety strikes, I'll breathe deeply and remind myself that it will pass.

Guilt is not my friend. I must find ways to show it the door.

I will ask forgiveness and also forgive myself, so I can be free to love you and grieve well.

I will say to myself, "I forgive you." This is part of loving and honoring you.

Blaming won't bring you back. Instead, I'll forgive. I want my heart as free as possible.

I know I need to build a new life, but I'm not ready yet. I'm too busy missing you. For now, I'll take things one step at a time, one moment at a time.

When I'm angry with God, I'll be honest about it. He can handle my emotions.

I'll grieve well by getting the time alone I need while staying connected to people who are helpful to me.

I'll try to eat well and take care of myself. You would want this.

Grief is exhausting. I'll try to have realistic expectations of myself during this time.

I will be myself and express my heart with those I trust and feel safe with. I will honor you by sharing my grief.

I'll recognize that your departure changes all our family relationships. This is stressful and confusing. I'll be patient with myself and all of us in this process.

If I discover something I didn't know that disturbs me, I will guard my heart. I will be honest with myself and try to process that information well.

I not only lost you but much of what was attached to you. I will be kind to myself because this is hard.

I can't expect others to understand my grief, but I will work to find some who will be respectful and considerate.

Grief is hitting my body too. I'll be kind to myself and take the best care of myself possible.

When unhelpful, insensitive words are said, I will protect my heart and release them as quickly as possible.

Some will try to fix me and my grief. I will remember that their words are usually more about them than about me.

I miss you and long to hear your voice. I love you.

I will be proactive and make a simple plan for your birthday. I will honor you and express my love.

I will be proactive and plan for how I will handle the grief bursts that come.

I will engage in life today as best as I can, remembering you.

I will find people who will listen and walk this grief road with me.

I'll release guilt and forgive myself as many times as necessary. Grief is heavy enough.

What I believe might be shaken or undergo some intense examination. This is natural.

Even if I feel empty and apathetic, I'll be patient with myself. I trust this will change over time.

I will accept myself and trust that any depression I experience is temporary and will pass with time.

If my depression deepens, I'll reach out for help. This is part of loving myself, and you.

I'll find ways to express my grief without comparing my loss to that of others. Comparison does not help me grieve well.

Life is tough and losing you is painful. There's plenty to scream about.

It's hard to imagine a future without you in it. I will focus on grieving well and celebrating you along the way.

I can't control the words and actions of others. I'll focus on grieving and being the best me possible in this situation.

Even if others don't mention you, I will. I'll give us a chance to grieve together.

Since I now know grief, I can engage with other grieving hearts. This could be good for all involved.

Even though I'm hurting, I can comfort others. My pain has purpose.

With family, I'll open my heart to those who are supportive and limit my exposure to those who aren't.

Grieving is a process. I'll be patient with myself and accept myself along the way.

If I feel less connected to you, I won't panic. This is part of grief.

I will speak your name and tell your story. This helps me grieve and is part of loving myself and you.

When fear of more loss comes, I'll acknowledge the fear and release it. This is part of grieving and living well.

When grief bursts come, I will breathe deeply and feel them through. These times are steps forward, not backward.

Rather than dreading special days, I will make plans to remember and honor you. This is part of loving myself and you.

My heart needs to continually express itself to be healthy and to heal. I'll find a way to do this.

I will live and love today, one person, one moment at a time.

Losing you has taught me I can look back, own the hurt I've caused, and live more meaningfully than ever before.

I can express simple kindness to other grieving hearts. This helps all of us.

Part of grieving is learning to let go of what is no longer helpful. I want to travel light and make a difference.

Letting go may not be what I thought. I can release what was and embrace what is, one moment at a time.

I'll keep breathing deeply, try to control less, and practice living in the present moment.

Losing you has sensitized me to the pain of other people. Even while hurting, I can comfort others.

Now that I know grief, I can be part of the solution for other grieving hearts. I will show up, listen, and love.

I will be patient with myself and remember that grief bursts can happen at any time, even months or years down the road.

I will make the anniversary of your leaving count. It will be hard, but it can still be good.

Loss has taught me what's important and how to live with more purpose and impact. I'm grateful for this.

I will make your loss count. I will love and live life one interaction, one moment at a time.

Help us reach other grieving parents and grandparents.
Share this link with others:
https://www.garyroe.com/comfort-series/

ALSO FOR BEREAVED PARENTS AND GRANDPARENTS

Shattered: Surviving the Loss of a Child

"A truly healing book."
Glen Lord, bereaved parent,
President/CEO, The Grief Toolbox;
President,Board of Directors, The Compassionate Friends

Unthinkable. Unbelievable. Heartbreaking.

Whatever words we choose, they all fall far short of the reality. The loss of a child is a terrible thing. How do we survive this? Can we?*Shattered: Surviving the Loss of a Child* was written to help.

Bestselling author, hospice chaplain, and grief specialist Gary Roe uses his three decades of experience interacting with grieving parents to give us this heartfelt, easy-to-read, and intensely practical book. In *Shattered*, Roe walks the reader through the powerful impact a child's death can have - emotionally, mentally, physically, relationally, and spiritually:

- Intense, unpredictable emotions can hijack us at a moment's notice.
- Our minds spin. We forget things. It feels like we're going crazy.
- Our bodies get hit. Our health can be impacted.
- Our souls feel crushed, shaking our faith and what we think we believe.
- Our relationships change. A deep loneliness of the heart can set in.
- Our plans and dreams are shattered. We're now in uncharted territory.

Yes, the loss of a child affects everything.

In *Shattered*, you will discover how to…

- Manage the massive changes that are occurring in your life
- Take care of yourself during this process
- Honor your child with your grief
- Love those around you, even with a broken heart
- Live life as well as possible while in the midst of great pain
- Make your child's life count in deep and powerful ways

Shattered is not a magic pill. The death of a child cannot be fixed. But comfort, compassion, guidance, and hope can be found in these pages.

We will never be the same, but we can survive. And to some degree, we can heal. *Shattered* can help.

"Few people truly comprehend the unique and challenging grief experiences of bereaved parents. Yet Gary Roe not only understands but also offers hope, healing, and compassion. As a bereaved parent and also as a professional who has worked with bereaved parents, I would highly recommend Shattered."

-Peggy Telg,
bereaved parent, Independent Bereavement Educator

"There isn't a book that can be written to explain exactly how we feel, but Shattered is no doubt the closest I've seen. Thanks to Gary Roe for helping us speak and giving our shattered lives a voice."

-Michelle Jeter, bereaved parent

"In Shattered, Gary Roe uniquely and delicately addresses the devastating subject of losing a child. This book will be an excellent resource, not only for bereaved parents, but also for those who support them."

- Joangeli Kasper,
Licensed Professional Counselor

"Shattered is superb. I believe that anyone could read it and find help with their grief after losing a child. It is a thorough, timely, and much needed book that could also be used as an excellent grief counseling reference manual."

- Dr. Tony Taylor,
Senior Pastor, Hilltop Lakes Chapel

Shattered is a Best Book Awards Finalist and is available in various formats through most major online book retailers.
www.garyroe.com/shattered

A FREE GIFT FOR YOU

CRISIS:
7 Principles for Uncertain Times

www.garyroe.com/crisis

Something happens, and our world is upended.

Life is not what it was, and we don't know what it will be. We're stuck in the middle - the limbo-land of uncertainty.

How do we navigate this new, uncharted territory we find ourselves in?

Written during the 2020 COVID-19 pandemic, this easy-to-read book outlines seven crucial principles for emotional, mental, physical, and spiritual health during times of unpredictability, stress, and upheaval.

These principles are timeless and can be applied to any crisis you might face in life.

Download your free copy of CRISIS today:
www.garyroe.com/crisis

ADDITIONAL RESOURCES

BOOKS

Aftermath: Picking Up the Pieces After a Suicide

Painful. Traumatic. Confusing. Complicated. No chance to say goodbye. No final embrace, kiss, or touch. No opportunity to clear the air, ask and give forgiveness, or make amends. The suicide tsunami has come, and now you're left standing amid the aftermath. This book is designed to be a companion for those grieving a suicide death, offering comfort, perspective, hope, and healing. Gary walks with you through all the emotional, mental, physical, spiritual, and relational upheaval that comes with a suicide loss. Let Gary journey with you through the aftermath and help you pick up the pieces and begin to rebuild your heart and life. *Aftermath* is available in various formats from most book retailers. **www.garyroe.com/aftermath**

Difference Maker: Overcoming Adversity and Turning Pain into Purpose, Every Day

You've been hit and wounded. Life hasn't turned out to be what you expected, wanted, or hoped for. Your heart says, "There's got to be more." Yes, there is. It's time to turn things around, expose the lies you've been fed about yourself, and embrace the truth. You're a Difference Maker. And it's time to start living that way. In *Difference Maker*, you'll discover how to conquer obstacles like fear, anxiety, anger, depression, self-destructive behavior, and suicidal thoughts. You'll learn why you're here, what your mission is, and how to live with more purpose and passion than you dreamed possible. *Difference Maker* is available in adult and teen editions in various formats from most online book distributors. The world needs you. Accept the Difference Maker challenge. **www.garyroe.com/difference-maker**

Teen Grief: Caring for the Grieving Teenage Heart

Teens are hurting. While trying to make sense of an increasingly confusing and troubled world, teens get hit, again and again. Edgy, fun-loving, tech-driven, and seemingly indestructible, their souls are shaking. We can't afford to allow pain and loss to get the better of them. What can we do? Written at the request of parents, teachers, coaches, and school counselors, this informative, practical book is replete with guidance, insight, and ideas for assisting teens navigate the turbulent waters of loss. As they heal and grow, they can become the Difference Makers this world so desperately needs. Winner of the Book Excellence Award, *Teen Grief* has received rave reviews from those who live and work with teens. *Teen Grief* is available in various formats from most book retailers. **www.garyroe.com/teengrief**

Please Be Patient, I'm Grieving: How to Care for and Support the Grieving Heart

People often feel misunderstood, judged, and even rejected during a time of loss. This makes matters more difficult for an already broken heart. It doesn't have to be this way. It's time we took the grieving heart seriously. Gary wrote this book by request to help others better understand and support grieving hearts and to help grieving hearts understand themselves. A group discussion guide is included. Please Be Patient, I'm Grieving was a Best Book Awards Finalist and can be found in various formats at most online bookstores. **www.garyroe.com/please-be-patient**

Heartbroken: Healing from the Loss of a Spouse

Losing a spouse is painful, confusing, and often traumatic. This comforting and practical book was penned from the stories of dozens of widows and widowers. It's simple, straightforward approach has emotionally impacted hearts and helped thousands know they're not alone, not crazy, and that they will make it. *Heartbroken* was a USA Best Book Award Finalist and a National Indie Excellence Book Award Finalist. Available in various formats from most major online retailers. **www.garyroe.com/heartbroken-2**

Surviving the Holidays Without You: Navigating Loss During Special Seasons

This warm and intensely practical volume has been dubbed a "Survival Kit for Holidays." It has helped many understand why holidays are especially hard while grieving and how to navigate them with greater confidence. Being proactive and having a plan can make all the difference. *Surviving the Holidays Without You* was a Book Excellence Award Finalist and is available in various formats from most major online retailers.
www.garyroe.com/surviving-the-holidays

Saying Goodbye: Facing the Loss of a Loved One

Full of stories, this warm, easy-to-read, and beautifully illustrated gift book has comforted thousands. It reads like a conversation with a close friend giving wise counsel and hope to those facing a loss. Co-authored with New York Times' Bestseller Cecil Murphey, this attractive hardback edition is available at **www.garyroe.com/saying-goodbye**

FREE ON GARY'S WEBSITE

The Good Grief Mini-Course

Full of personal stories, inspirational content, and practical assignments, this 8-session email series is designed to help readers understand grief and deal with its roller-coaster emotions. Several thousand have been through this course, which is now being used in support groups as well.
Available at **www.garyroe.com**.

The Hole in My Heart: Tackling Grief's Tough Questions

This e-book tackles some of grief 's big questions: "How did this happen?" "Why?" "Am I crazy?" "Am I normal?" "Will this get any easier?" plus others. Written in the first person, it engages and comforts the heart. Available at **www.garyroe.com**.

I Miss You: A Holiday Survival Kit

Thousands have downloaded this brief, easy-to-read, and very personal e-book. I Miss You provides some basic, simple tools on how to use holiday and special times to grieve well and love those around you.
Available at **www.garyroe.com**.

A REQUEST FROM THE AUTHOR

Thank you for taking your heart seriously and reading *Comfort for the Grieving Parent's Heart.* I hope you found some comfort, healing, and practical help in its pages.

I would love to hear what you thought of the book. Would you consider taking a moment and sending me a few sentences on how *Comfort for the Grieving Parent's Heart* impacted you?

Send me your thoughts at **contact@garyroe.com**.

Your comments and feedback mean a lot to me and will assist me in producing more quality resources for grieving hearts.

Thank you.

Warmly,

Gary

Help us reach other grieving parents.

Share this link:

https://www.garyroe.com/comfort-series/

CARING FOR GRIEVING HEARTS

Visit Gary at www.garyroe.com and connect with him on Facebook, Twitter, LinkedIn, and Pinterest

Links:

Facebook: **https://www.facebook.com/garyroeauthor**

Twitter: **https://twitter.com/GaryRoeAuthor**

LinkedIn: **https://www.linkedin.com/in/garyroeauthor**

Pinterest: **https://www.pinterest.com/garyroe79/**

ABOUT THE AUTHOR

Gary's story began with a childhood of mixed messages and sexual abuse. This was followed by other losses and numerous grief experiences.

Ultimately, a painful past led Gary into a life of helping wounded people heal and grow. A former college minister, missionary in Japan, entrepreneur in Hawaii, and pastor in Texas and Washington, he now serves as a writer, speaker, chaplain, and grief counselor.

In addition to *Comfort for the Grieving Parent's Heart,* Gary is the author of numerous books, including the award-winning bestsellers *Shattered: Surviving the Loss of a Child, Comfort for the Grieving Spouse's Heart,* and *Aftermath: Picking Up the Pieces After a Suicide.* Gary's books have won two national book awards and have been named as finalists seven times. He has been featured on Dr. Laura, Belief Net, the Christian Broadcasting Network, Wellness, Thrive Global, and other major media and has well over 700 grief-related articles in print. Recipient of the Diane Duncam Award for Excellence in Hospice Care, Gary is a popular keynote, conference, and seminar speaker at a wide variety of venues.

Gary loves being a husband and father. He has seven adopted children, including three daughters from Colombia. He enjoys hockey, corny jokes, good puns, and colorful Hawaiian shirts. Gary and his wife Jen and family live in Texas.

Visit Gary at www.garyroe.com.
Download your exclusive, free, printable PDF:
Healing Affirmations for Grieving Hearts
https://www.garyroe.com/healing-affirmations-for-grieving-hearts/

ACKNOWLEDGEMENTS

Special thanks for my lovely wife, Jen for her constant and unwavering support and encouragement. Thank you for engaging with me in giving hope and bringing healing.

Special thanks to Peggy Sanders, Kathy Trim, Anni Welborne, and Kelli Levey Reynolds for their keen proofreading eyes and editorial assistance. I appreciate you more than you know.

Thanks to Dr. Craig Borchardt of Hospice Brazos Valley for his continued support in producing quality resources for grieving hearts. It's an honor to work under your supervision.

Thanks to Glendon Haddix of Streetlight Graphics for his artistic skill and expertise in design and formatting. Your artistry continues to bring healing and hope to many.

AN URGENT PLEA

HELP OTHER GRIEVING HEARTS

Dear Reader,

Others are hurting and grieving today. You can help.

How?

With a simple, heartfelt review.

Could you take a few moments and write a 1-3 sentence review of *Comfort for the Grieving Parent's Heart* and leave it on the site you purchased the book from?

And if you want to help even more, you could leave the same review on the *Comfort for the Grieving Parent's Heart* book page on Goodreads.

Your review counts and will help reach others who could benefit from this book.

Thanks for considering this. I read these reviews as well, and your comments and feedback assist me in producing more quality resources for grieving hearts.

Thank you!

Warmly,

Gary

Made in the USA
Las Vegas, NV
08 November 2022

58894370R00164